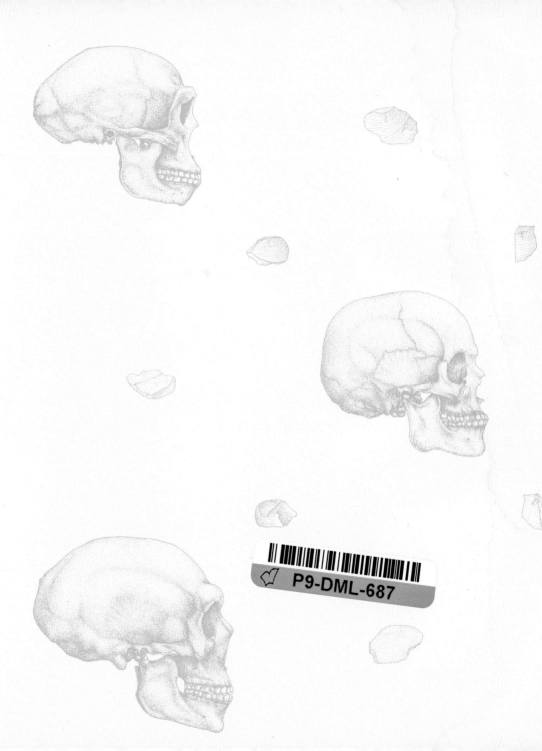

# SMITHSONIAN INTIMATE GUIDE TO HUMAN ORIGINS

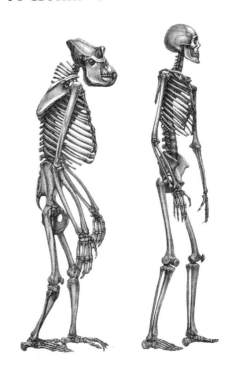

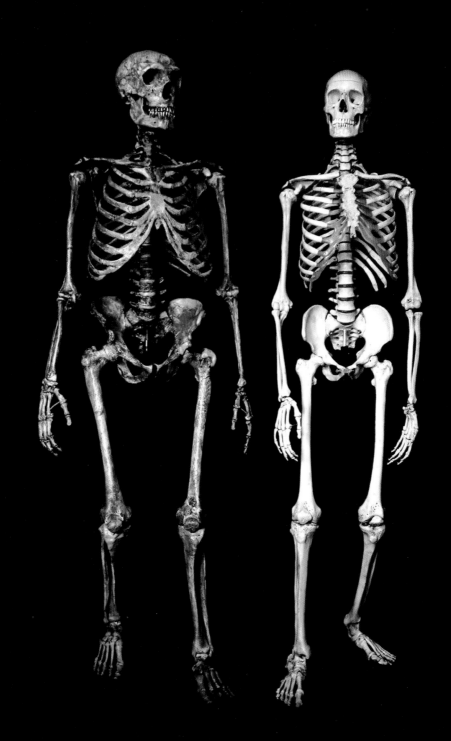

SMITHSONIAN INTIMATE GUIDE TO

# HUMAN ORIGINS

CARL ZIMMER

Smithsonian Books

Collins
An Imprint of HarperCollinsPublishers

produced by MADISON PRESS BOOKS

FIRST EDITION

Library of Congress Cataloguing-in-Publication Data has been applied for.

ISBN-10: 0-06-082961-3
ISBN-13: 978-0-06-082961-2

Produced by Madison Press Books
1000 Yonge Street—Suite 200
Toronto, Ontario, Canada
M4W 2K2

Printed in Singapore

10  09  08  07  06  05
9  8  7  6  5  4  3  2  1

# Contents

# Bones, Tools and Genes:

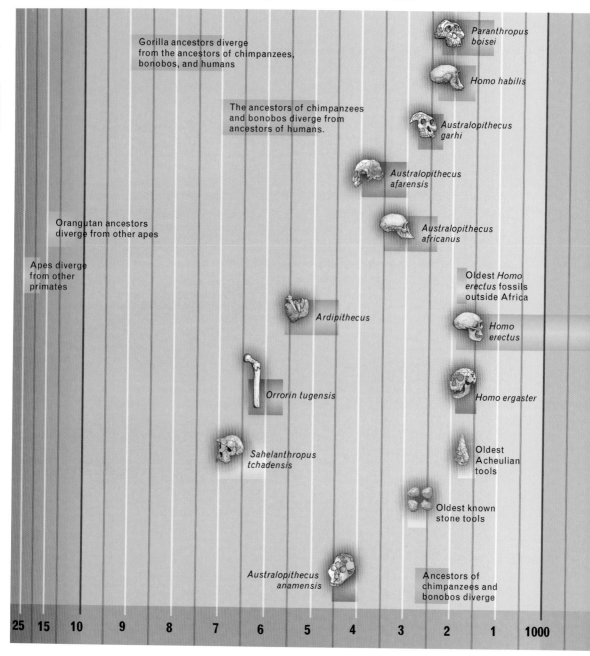

Gorilla ancestors diverge
from the ancestors of chimpanzees,
bonobos, and humans

The ancestors of chimpanzees
and bonobos diverge from
ancestors of humans.

Orangutan ancestors
diverge from other apes

Apes diverge
from other
primates

*Paranthropus
boisei*

*Homo habilis*

*Australopithecus
garhi*

*Australopithecus
afarensis*

*Australopithecus
africanus*

Oldest *Homo
erectus* fossils
outside Africa

*Ardipithecus*

*Homo
erectus*

*Orrorin tugensis*

*Homo ergaster*

Oldest
Acheulian
tools

*Sahelanthropus
tchadensis*

Oldest known
stone tools

*Australopithecus
anamensis*

Ancestors of
chimpanzees and
bonobos diverge

25  15  10  9  8  7  6  5  4  3  2  1  1000

**Millions of Years Ago**

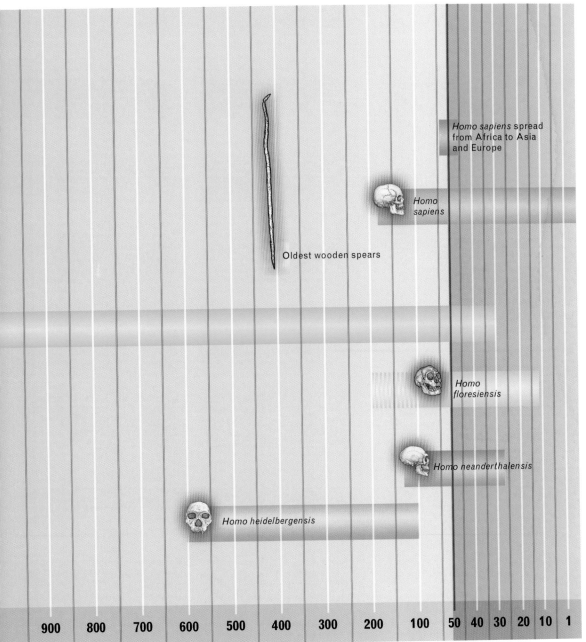

Homo sapiens spread
from Africa to Asia
and Europe

Homo
sapiens

Oldest wooden spears

Homo
floresiensis

Homo neanderthalensis

Homo heidelbergensis

900   800   700   600   500   400   300   200   100   50   40   30   20   10   1

**Thousands of Years Ago**

This chart shows some of the key species and evolutionary milestones in the history of
hominids. For clarity, the more recent portions of this chart have been expanded.

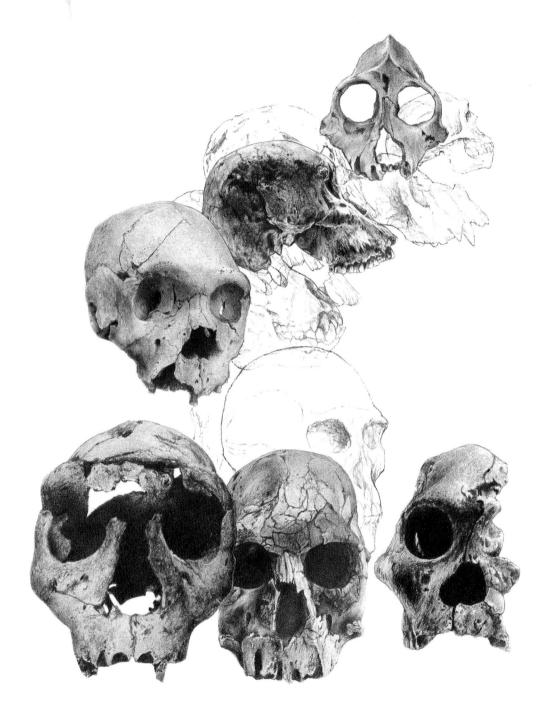

## CHAPTER ONE

# The Clues

The winds of the Sahara Desert sandblast the Earth. They scour rocks, stripping an inch-thick layer away every year. But not everything the winds touch is so easy to dislodge. Fossils of long-dead animals and plants resist, even as the soft sandstone surrounding them vanishes. Gradually the fossils emerge into sunlight after millions of years in darkness. Paleontologists try to rescue them during this fleeting moment of exposure. Before long, even the toughest fossil will melt away under the sandblasting winds, lost to science forever.

One team of paleontologists regularly visits a particularly bleak region of the Sahara called the Djurab, in northern Chad. Some of the scientists are French, some Chadian. Their tents are sometimes buried in sand; sometimes they have to wear ski masks to protect their faces from the scouring winds. They face human threats as well—private armies bury land mines in the area, and hold up the paleontologists at gunpoint.

The scientists search for fossils among sandstone formations that turned to rock six to seven million years ago, along the shores of an ancient lake. Today the Djurab sees hardly a drop of rain, but the paleontologists have discovered that six to seven million years ago, fish swam here along with crocodiles and frogs. Pythons slithered through the lakeside grasses, while turtles clambered in the mud. Trees and bushes formed a thick collar around the lake, attracting elephants, pigs, hippos, rodents and monkeys. Giraffes and horses grazed; big cats hunted; hyenas scavenged.

In 2001, a young university student named Ahounta Djimdoumalbaye found a peculiar skull exposed by the winds. It was smaller than a horse, bigger than a monkey. As Djimdoumalbaye and other members of the team scraped it out of the sandstone, its broad dome emerged, crowned by a ridge over two forward-facing eye sockets. Its face was flat and its front teeth were relatively small. These telltale clues revealed it to be part of our own close evolutionary family, more kin to humans than to chimpanzees or any other mammal. Paleontologists call such fossil species hominids. And this particular hominid, which the scientists dubbed *Sahelanthropus tchadensis,* is the oldest one yet found. It may belong to one of the earliest species that evolved after our lineage branched off from that of other apes.

Digging in the Sahara is not the only way scientists gather clues about human evolution. Some of the most important ones have been discovered in suburban Maryland, where robots at the National Human Genome Research Institute analyze DNA. Our genome hides genetic traces of our history, such as silenced genes that have not been able to produce proteins for millions of years. By comparing the human genome to those of other animals, scientists can trace the 600-million-year history of our brains. They are also isolating genes that changed dramatically in just the past 200,000 years, as our ancestors acquired the gifts—such as language—that make us uniquely human.

In addition to studying genomes and fossils, scientists can find clues about where we come from in other ways. MRI scans can give hints as to how the circuits of our brains were rewired over the past few million years. Supercomputers can re-create the shambling gait of our ancestors before they walked upright. But just as important as all this technology are the long, patient hours that primatologists spend watching our closest relatives—the chimpanzees and other apes. In their careful observations come new insights into the origins of human culture.

When you consider all of the ways scientists can study human evolution today, it's mind-boggling to think about how little Charles Darwin had to work with when he first began to think about our origins. Fossil spear-points and other stone tools had been known since the 1600s. Three years before Darwin published *The Origin of Species*, German quarry workers shoveled up a skullcap and a few other bones of Neanderthals. Today, most researchers consider Neanderthals a separate species of human that became extinct 28,000 years ago. But at the time, naturalists were baffled by the Neanderthal's almost-humanness. It seemed to be about the same size as a grown man, but its skull displayed a low, thick brow ridge. Thomas Huxley, one of Britain's leading naturalists, decided that

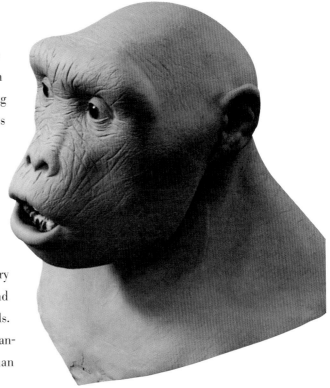

A reconstruction of *Sahelanthropus tchadensis*, the oldest known hominid. It features a mix of ape-like traits and other traits that link it to humans.

Neanderthals were not far beyond the range of variation found in living humans and made them members of our own species. "In no sense, then, can the Neanderthal bones be regarded as the remains of a human being intermediate between Men and Apes," he wrote in his 1863 book *Man's Place in Nature*.

# THE EVIDENCE

People knew of fossils for many centuries before anyone realized what they were. Without overwhelming evidence, who would believe that bones can turn to stone, or that they could survive for hundreds of millions of years? The realization might have come sooner if all fossils were exquisitely preserved down to the last toe, fin or tentacle. But, unfortunately, scientists are rarely so lucky. In fact, when it comes to animals such as hominids, scientists are lucky to find fossils at all. Only a tiny fraction of all the hominids that ever lived have been memorialized in rock.

What determined whether a hominid turned into a fossil or not? Its fate was largely decided by how it died. If a hominid was killed by a leopard, most of its bones would be digested, gnawed or otherwise destroyed. The remnants would be worked over by insects and bacteria, and finally washed away into a river and then the sea.

A better candidate for fossilization would have died by drowning in a still, muddy pool. Its body might then be gradually covered by sediment. As its flesh was devoured by mud-dwelling bacteria, its skeleton would remain joined together. Over the course of millions of years, the bones would be transformed to stone. This process is so slow

that the shape of the skeleton is not disturbed; fossils can preserve details of bone down to microscopic detail.

Even after this wonderful metamorphosis, a hominid skeleton may not survive. The Earth is restless, and the fossil might be destroyed by a planetary twitch. A river might begin to flow over the rocks that contain the fossil and erode it away. The grasslands overhead might turn to desert, and the sandblasting winds might expose the fossil and then grind it to dust.

If a hominid beats all these odds, an exposed end of its fossil just might catch the eye of an intrepid paleoanthropologist. What comes next is a slow, immensely patient excavation. Over millions of years, hominid fossils are typically reduced to hunks and chips of bone. In many cases, paleoanthropologists will simply dig out the entire rock and bring it back to a laboratory, where they can free each piece of the fossil while keeping careful track of the other pieces it was found with. A single fossil can take years to pull from the rock, but the payoff is enormous—a glimpse at our ancestry.

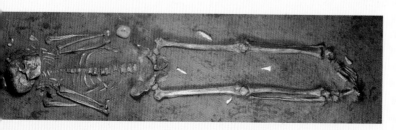

Top: Fish fossils from Wyoming.
Left: A fossil of a *Homo sapiens* child found in Italy.

In 1857 German quarry workers dug up these 40,000-year-old Neanderthal bones. It was the first time humans had discovered the bones of another species of hominid.

For fossils, that was about it. Genomes were unknown—DNA itself had yet to be discovered. Yet Charles Darwin still managed to recognize some of the basic processes that have shaped our species. Like other animals, humans pass on certain traits to their children. In each generation, these traits vary from one person to the next. Some people are tall; others, short; some are heavy; some, thin. Like other Victorians, Darwin knew very well that not all people manage to pass on their traits to the next generation. (Three of his ten children died before the age of ten.) If a trait helps a person survive and reproduce, it may, over time, become more common among our species. In other words, humans are just as subject to natural selection as any other species.

Charles Darwin contemplated human evolution for decades before publishing his ideas in
*The Descent of Man* in 1871.

Darwin argued that selection could cause a new species to branch off from an existing one. He saw these branches forming a tree of life, with new limbs continually budding off as old limbs were pruned by extinction. Humans, Darwin concluded, had emerged from this same tree of life. The closest branches to our own produced our closest living relatives—chimpanzees, gorillas and orangutans.

The uncanny similarities between humans and apes had been noted for over a century. In the 1690s, the English anatomist Edward Tyson performed the first dissection of a chimpanzee. In his 1699 book, *The Anatomy of a Pygmie*, he wrote that the chimp and the human brain bore a "surprising" resemblance, commenting that "one would be apt to think, that since there is so great a disparity between the Soul of a Man, and a Brute, the Organ likewise in which 'tis placed should be very different too."

Darwin mused for a long time about the similarities between humans and apes. He paid regular visits to the London Zoo to observe an orangutan named Jenny, taking notes about the similarity of her facial expressions to those of humans. But for years Darwin

Above: Seventeenth-century anatomists noticed how similar the chimpanzee brain was to the human brain.

Overleaf: A chimpanzee skull, left, compared to a human skull.

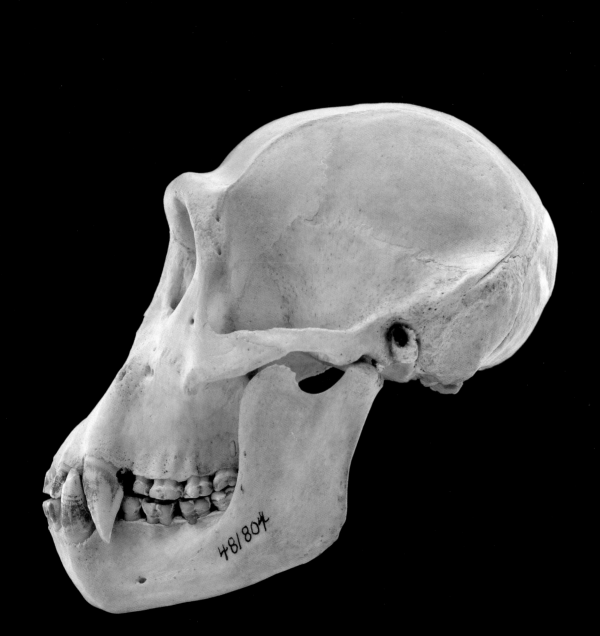
481804

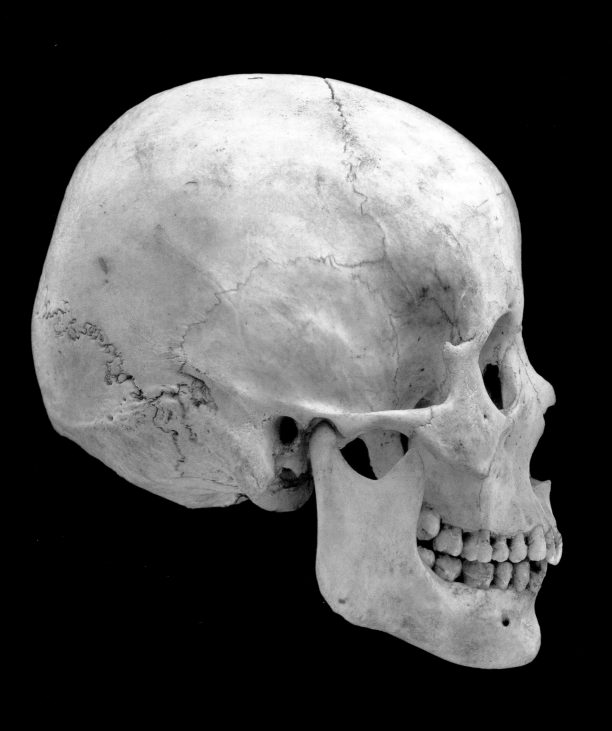

kept his ideas about human origins to himself. He filled *The Origin of Species* with enough animals to stock the London Zoo many times over. Whales, bears and flatworms parade through his pages, along with giant extinct sloths, armadillos and marine reptiles. But one species is glaringly absent: *Homo sapiens.* "Light will be thrown on the origin of man and his history," was all Darwin would say.

Darwin knew that it would be hard enough to persuade his readers that animals or plants evolved. To add humans to evolution's list of accomplishments might instantly turn them away. "I thought that I should thus only add to the prejudices against my views," he later wrote.

He was probably right. Most of the attacks launched against *The Origin of Species* sooner or later came around to the question of man's place in nature.

A gorilla skull at Down House, Charles Darwin's residence in the English countryside.

Richard Owen, the greatest British anatomist of the nineteenth century, thought he could refute evolution by finding a part of the brain that was unique to humans. Such a trait would set humans safely apart from other apes, and thus out of the grasp of Darwin's natural selection. In 1860, a year after the publication of *The Origin of Species*, Owen attended the most famous debate over Darwin, at Oxford University, where Bishop Samuel Wilberforce delivered a furious attack on *The Origin of Species*. He ended his speech by turning to Thomas Huxley and asking him whether he descended from an ape on his mother's or on his father's side.

As the years passed, however, the attacks faded. Naturalists still debated about how evolution worked. Did life have a built-in direction along which it evolved, they wondered, or was it nothing more than the adaptation of populations to the randomly changing conditions they faced? But all sides increasingly agreed that life had indeed evolved. Seeing a consensus emerging, Darwin decided the time was right to put humans in his zoo. In 1871 he published *The Descent of Man*, presenting evidence that humans had evolved and suggesting that they were modified mammals descended from an ape-like African ancestor.

Today, scientists have far more evidence at hand than Darwin had to test

Darwin was caricatured in the press in 1871, the year he published *The Descent of Man*.

ideas about human evolution. In many ways he has been splendidly vindicated. Fossils of hominids have been found dating as far back as six million years. For the first four million years of hominid ancestry, all known species lived in Africa, strongly supporting an African origin to our branch on the tree of life. But scientists have also discovered many things that would surprise Darwin. For example, Darwin thought that as the ancestors of humans evolved bipedalism, they evolved large brains at the same time. But fossils suggest that the first hominids to stand upright had brains one-third the size of a human's. It took four million years before their descendants would evolve a brain approaching the size of our own.

Despite recent insights into our origins, there is much we still don't know. That's not unusual in science. Physicists, for example, may have plumbed the atom but the fundamental nature of gravity still eludes them. And compared to scientists who study human evolution, physicists are drowning in information. To understand how an electron works, they can run experiments over and over again, studying the behavior of trillions of particles. History, on the other hand, is an experiment that runs only once. Still, scientists can test hypotheses about evolution by surveying the different forms life has taken on its different branches. They can search for ancient relics carried down from one generation to the next in DNA. And they can study the fossils of extinct species.

Making matters worse, our species has a history that's particularly hard to reconstruct. At first this might seem odd, since we belong to a very young lineage. The earliest evidence of life on Earth—a balance of chemicals in ancient rocks that could have been formed only by biological organisms—dates back 3.7 billion years. The common ancestor that humans share with chimpanzees lived only six to seven million years ago. If the history of life were squeezed into a single day, that common ancestor would have been born three minutes before midnight.

The oldest fossils known to belong to our own species, *Homo sapiens*, date back 195,000 years—only five seconds before the end of the day.

While our hominid roots may not run very deep, the mysteries of our evolution remain vast. Part of the problem is that hominids are particularly rare in the fossil record. They never formed great herds, nor did they live in the sorts of places where fossils have a good chance to be preserved. The unique features of our species make the task even more challenging. Of all living animals, only humans can use full-blown language and only humans have true consciousness. Scientists are just beginning to understand how our brains make all this possible, yet these traits leave little mark on the fossil record.

While scientists will never recover a perfect picture of human evolution, their success in recent years makes it a safe bet that they will continue to make astonishing new discoveries for years to come. Perhaps Darwin said it best: "It has often and confidently been asserted, that man's origin can never be known," he wrote in *The Descent of Man*. "But ignorance more frequently begets confidence than does knowledge. It is those who know little, and not those who know much, who so positively assert that this or that problem will never be solved by science."

Darwin's thoughts on human evolution continue to influence paleoanthropologists today.

# Telling Time

Darwin recognized that time was at the heart of evolution. Lots of time. Natural selection might only produce subtle changes in a single generation, but if thousands or millions of generations had lived, its effects could be profound. In the mid-1800s, when Darwin was working out his theory of evolution, scientists had only the dimmest conception of how old the Earth was. Geologists were beginning to appreciate that the rocks of the planet had formed very slowly, either from volcanic eruptions or the steady settling of sediments in coastal waters. Most agreed that the process took a long time, but few could say how long.

Precision came to geological dating in the twentieth century, thanks to radioactivity. When rocks form, they sometimes contain trace levels of radioactive elements, such as uranium. Over time, these unstable atoms break down into other elements. Physicists have found that they decay at regular rates. Half the uranium-238 in a rock will be left in 4.47 billion years; half of the remaining uranium will be left in 4.47 billion years more, and so on. To describe this decline, physicists say the half-life of uranium-238 is 4.47 billion years.

Radiometric dating gave the world a time scale. By comparing the uranium in rocks from Earth to rocks from meteorites, the American geologist Claire Patterson discovered in the 1950s that the planet is 4.5 billion years old. Geologists can also use radiometric dating to calculate the age of individual rocks. They can put the most precise dates on rocks that formed during volcanic eruptions, because these rocks are relatively rich in radioactive elements.

Paleoanthropologists can use the dates of volcanic eruptions to put brackets on the age of fossils they discover. Say that a volcano blankets southern Ethiopia with ash 160,000 years ago. The ash is overgrown with grass and trees, and then many centuries later a human happens to die on the same spot. His skeleton happens to fossilize, and then, 156,000 years ago, another eruption blankets the same place with ash. Today the layers of rock created by those eruptions form a sandwich between the sediments that hold the fossils. If paleoanthropologists dig up the fossil, they can use the precise dates determined for the volcanic layers to conclude that the sandwiched hominid lived between 156,000 and 160,000 years ago. This was actually what happened to some of the oldest known fossils of *Homo sapiens*, which we will encounter in Chapter 6.

Paleoanthropologists are not always so lucky, though. Some hominid fossils are found in layers of rock that are not closely sandwiched by volcanic eruptions. Such was the case with *Sahelanthropus*. Michel Brunet and his colleagues had to

resort instead to a rougher method. They took advantage of the fact that species themselves can act as timekeepers. A typical species—be it a bird, a fish or a snai — exists only for a few million years at most, and usually occupies a small range. Once scientists can bracket the "lifespan" of a species with radiometric dates of volcanic rocks, its fossil can offer a guide to the age of other rocks that can't be dated with radioactive clocks. For example, extinct, fish-like vertebrates called con-odonts left behind vast numbers of tooth-shaped elements that are distinctive enough to let paleon-tologists identify the species of conodont, and then calculate its lifespan.

Brunet's team used a similar method to esti-

Opposite: A conodont, an ancient vertebrate. Its abundant fossils help geologists estimate the ages of rocks. Above: Single-celled marine creatures called foraminifera also act as geological clocks.

mate the age of *Sahelanthropus*. Alongside the hominid's fossil, the researchers found a wealth of fossil bones from other animal species. Several of the same species are also found together in other sites in Africa, where their fossils happened to have formed either before or after volcanic eruptions. Based on the ages of these species, the researchers estimate that *Sahelanthropus* must have lived between six and seven million years ago.

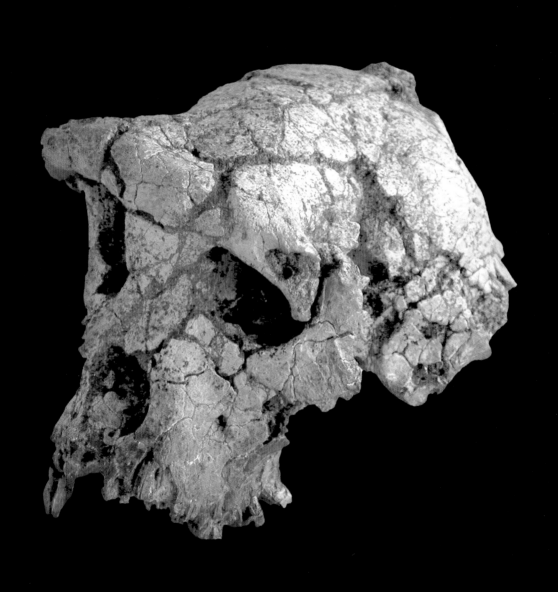

## CHAPTER TWO

# A BUDDING BRANCH

When the world was first introduced to *Sahelanthropus tchadensis* in 2002, many experts hailed it as the greatest discovery in paleoanthropology in seventy-five years. *Sahelanthropus*'s crushed skull appeared on the front pages of newspapers and the covers of magazines. The leader of the team that found it, Michel Brunet of the University of Poitiers, France, had previously been a relatively obscure paleontologist, and perfectly happy that way. Suddenly he was as famous as his fossil—hounded for autographs, feted by presidents.

It's not hard to understand why Brunet became a celebrity. We are obsessed with the beginnings of things. The oldest known species in our own lineage can't help but inspire attention. But along the way, people came to see *Sahelanthropus* as the Rosetta Stone of human nature—a profound misunderstanding about how scientists study human evolution. Their goal is not actually to find the oldest hominid. *Sahelanthropus* is indeed a spectacular discovery, but on its own it says practically nothing about how we got to be the way we are now. That's because evolution can't be summed up in a single species, let alone in a single fossil.

Consider, for example, *Sahelanthropus*'s eyes. The sockets in its skull face forward, meaning that when it was alive, it had binocular vision. We humans have binocular vision as well, and it's an important element to our existence. Because

*Sahelanthropus tchadensis*, discovered in the Sahara Desert in 2001, is between six and seven million years old. It is generally considered the oldest known hominid fossil.

both eyes point forward, they focus on a central point in front of our face. And because each eye has a slightly different perspective on the same object, our brain can compare the differences, and this gives us a keen sense of depth. Our eyes can extract a great deal of information from this focal point, because its image falls on a tiny patch of the retina crammed with light-sensitive nerve endings. Thanks in part to our forward-facing eyes, we can use our hands to carry out delicate, complex tasks. To appreciate just how important they are, just imagine going to the hospital for brain surgery. You wouldn't be happy to find that your surgeon had eyes like a pigeon, pointing out from the sides of his head.

Are *Sahelanthropus*'s forward-facing eyes the key to the evolution of this trait? Hardly. Our evolutionary heritage reaches back far beyond *Sahelanthropus*. We share a common ancestor with all living things on Earth, from bacteria to aardvarks. Our closest relatives are primates—apes, monkeys, lemurs and such—and we share a common ancestor with them that lived about sixty-five million years ago. This common ancestor had binocular vision, as evidenced by the fact that all living primates have it as well. The fact that *Sahelanthropus* had forward-facing eyes simply means that it inherited this trait from a long line of ancestors, along with its ears, teeth, hands and feet. The evolutionary forces that first produced binocular vision were at work tens of millions of years before *Sahelanthropus* existed. Only when it is put alongside other species can *Sahelanthropus* help reveal the story of our evolution.

We could start this story 3.7 billion years ago with the earliest microbes, but let's save a few hundred pages and just jump ahead to the end of the Cretaceous Period, sixty-five million years ago. The age of reptiles was coming to an end. For 135 million years, dinosaurs had been the dominant land animals. Their close reptilian cousins, pterosaurs, flapped through the air on bristly, membranous wings. Whale-sized marine reptiles glided through the oceans.

These reptiles suffered catastrophic extinctions at the end of the Cretaceous Period, probably due to the impact of a ten-mile-wide asteroid in the Gulf of Mexico. The tidal waves, forest fires, acid rain and darkened skies wiped out half of all species on Earth. Some lineages of reptiles survived—the alligators, the lizards and snakes, the turtles and the birds. Frogs and other amphibians endured the catastrophe as well. But in many ways the age that followed would belong to another group of animals that, until the end of the Cretaceous, could have been easy to overlook: the mammals.

The ancestors of mammals branched off from the ancestors of reptiles over 300 million years ago. In the early years, the forerunners of mammals were lumbering, lizard-like creatures, but by 200 million years ago, they had given rise to true mammals—small, hairy animals that produced milk for their young and could maintain a warm body temperature. The first mammals probably hunted insects and the like, perhaps at night or at dusk. Throughout the age of reptiles, they remained tiny, rarely evolving beyond the size of a cat. And yet, despite the similarity of mammals at the end of the Cretaceous Period, they had already diverged into the major groups that are still found on Earth today. One of those groups was our own, the primates.

The oldest fossils of primates date back to the Paleocene Period, which immediately followed the asteroid impact sixty-five million years ago. These early primates, ranging from the size of a shrew to that of a cat, had already adapted to life in the trees. They could climb

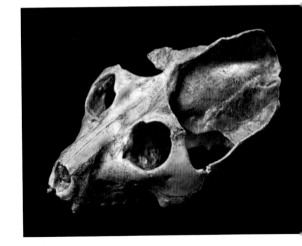

*Adapis*, which lived fifty million years ago, is one of the oldest known primates. It resembled a small lemur.

# What is DNA?

Within each cell of your body is a genetic cookbook for building a human being. Scientists refer to this cookbook as a genome. It is composed of a single molecule, known as DNA, which consists of two twisted strands. Each of those strands carries a series of compounds, called nucleotides, that you can think of as the letters in the genome's cookbook. Instead of twenty-six letters in the regular alphabet, there are only four different nucleotides in DNA. A human genome is over three billion nucleotides long—a sequence long enough to fill thousands of books.

The genome contains recipes for building proteins, the basic components of the body. Some of the estimated 100,000 human proteins give the body structure, while others carry out the chemical reactions that make life possible—ferrying oxygen through the blood, for example, or digesting food. The building blocks for proteins are twenty compounds known as amino acids. The instructions for building each protein are carried in a sequence of DNA known as a gene. Each gene is several thousand nucleotides long. Special DNA-reading proteins use a gene's sequence as a template for assembling amino acids together. Scientists estimate that there are 20,000 to 25,000 genes in the human genome. By reading different sections of a single gene, our cells can produce several different proteins.

A mutation to a gene can cause it to stop producing proteins, or to produce a protein with a different structure. Most mutations are harmful or have no effect on an individual. A few, however, may prove to be beneficial. If mutations tend to boost the number of offspring an individual has, they will spread through a population. This is the core of natural selection—a process something like updating a cookbook.

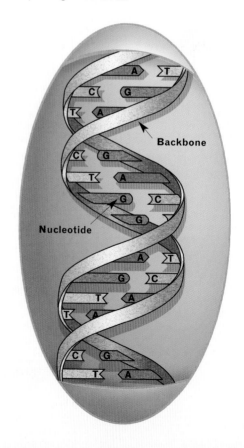

A diagram of DNA. The abbreviations stand for the four nucleotides. A: adenine; C: cytosine; G: guanine; T: thymine.

nimbly on branches, probably sniffing for fruit and insects. But only a trained paleontologist would recognize the subtle features of their teeth and ear bones that mark them as relatives of monkeys and apes. To the rest of us, they'd look like squirrels. By fifty-five million years ago these primates had given rise to new species with much of the anatomy seen in primates today. Their snouts shrank, and their eyes moved to the front of their faces. They were shifting from a world of smells to one of sights, and their brains shifted as well, with more space dedicated to processing vision. Studies on primate DNA show that the two main living branches emerged around this time. One lineage gave rise to lorises and lemurs. The other primate branch gave rise to the majority of living primate species, including monkeys, apes and us.

These early primates left fossils behind in many parts of the world. They even lived in Wyoming. They could thrive so far from the equator because the world's climate at the time was very warm. High levels of carbon dioxide in the atmosphere trapped heat, helping to raise the average global temperature and support high-latitude tropical forests where primates could live. But these balmy days were running out.

Over millions of years, the atmosphere's levels of carbon dioxide gradually fell. Many geologists suspect that the birth of the Himalayas and the Tibetan Plateau about forty million years ago had something to do with it. Carbon dioxide combined with the silica exposed on the new mountain slopes, and was then carried down to the ocean. Once this carbon became buried in the sea floor, less carbon was available to enter the atmosphere. With a lower level of carbon dioxide, the atmosphere cooled. Tropical forests vanished from places like Wyoming, and primates began to disappear from many of their old ranges. As we'll see in later chapters, Earth's climate has continued to change, and those changes have continued to shape human evolution.

One of the places where primates could still thrive was Africa, and it was there, roughly twenty-five million years ago, that a new lineage of primates emerged: the apes. Apes probably evolved from small, monkey-like ancestors that walked on branches using both hands and feet. They most likely held their backs horizontally and extended their long tails for balance. Over time, apes grew large, with early fossils indicating they weighed between 20 and 170 pounds. Instead of walking on all fours in trees, they began to use their arms to grab overhead branches, holding their backs vertically. Perhaps they also used their arms to reach for fruits. No longer balancing themselves over a branch, they relied less on their tails. Mutations gradually reduced their tails to a hidden vestige at the base of their spine—a vestige humans and other living apes still carry today. The early apes diversified into a wide range of forms. Some may have been able to walk nearly upright. Others clambered through trees using hands and feet, like baboons. While some apes may have spent time on the ground, most appear to have dwelled in the forest canopy.

Apes spread out of Africa into the Middle East and onward to Europe and Asia. Today, only a few remnants of this evolutionary burst survive, but the DNA of living apes preserves clues about their distant origins. Gibbons, which branched off about eighteen million years ago, swing through the trees of southeast Asia. After gibbons split off, the ancestors of the other living apes evolved to much bigger

An artist's rendition of *Gigantopithecus blacki*, an enormous extinct ape believed to be related to orangutans.

sizes (which is why their living descendants are called the great apes). Of all the great apes, orangutans are our most distant relatives, their ancestors having branched off from our own twelve to fifteen million years ago. The lineage that ultimately produced living orangutans also produced several other Asian apes that are now extinct. One of the strangest, known as *Gigantopithecus*, left behind some enormous teeth that have led paleoanthropologists to estimate that it would have stood ten feet high and weighed 1200 pounds. Today orangutans are the only survivors of this twelve-million-year-old dynasty. At the rate that their Indonesian forests are disappearing under the saws of loggers, they may soon become extinct as well.

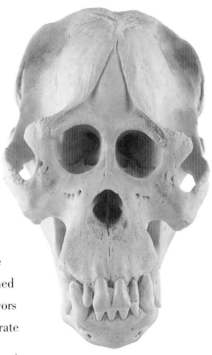

An orangutan skull. The common ancestor of orangutans and humans is estimated to have lived between twelve and fifteen million years ago.

DNA studies indicate that the next great branching took place at some point seven to nine million years ago, when our lineage split from the ancestors of gorillas. Later, our ancestors branched off from our closest living relatives, the chimpanzees and bonobos. Initially these two apes were considered a single species, but in the middle of the twentieth century zoologists noticed that those living in the southern Congo were visibly different from other populations, with a slimmer frame and darker skin. Later, scientists recognized that their societies were different as well. Chimpanzee society is centered around males, with females leaving their parents' troop to join new ones. In bonobo society, the females rule.

Bonobos (*Pan paniscus*), above, were once thought to belong to the same species as chimpanzees (*Pan troglodytes*). Now scientists estimate that the last common ancestor of chimpanzees and bonobos lived over two million years ago.

In the 1990s, when scientists began to study the DNA of these apes, they confirmed the split. Bonobos and chimpanzees belong to two separate branches, which diverged over two million years ago. Trace their ancestry back farther, and you reach a common ancestor with humans. DNA studies indicate that the ancestor of chimpanzees, bonobos and humans lived five to seven million years ago. (It can be a little confusing to think of two species as our closest living relatives. Imagine them as members of our extended family, which, ultimately, they are. In the primate family, you can think of bonobos and chimpanzees as sisters who are both our first cousins.)

While the evidence from living apes tells us a lot about our origins, it's easy to read too much into it. Just because our closest living relatives are chimpanzees and bonobos doesn't mean that we descend from chimpanzees or bonobos. Neither species existed seven million years ago. Neither chimpanzees nor bonobos can act as stand-ins for their common ancestor with humans. After their ancestors diverged from our own, chimpanzees and bonobos acquired new traits that we humans do not share. You need only to look at the DNA of chimpanzees for proof. Its genome contains many sequences not found in humans or any other living ape. Our relationship with chimpanzees, on its own, can't answer questions about our common ancestor, such as how it walked. It's possible, for example, that living chimpanzees knuckle-walk in the same way our common ancestor did. But it's also possible that the common ancestor of chimpanzees and humans lived in the trees, and each species later evolved its own way of walking.

Fossils could bring our picture of that common ancestor into sharper focus. Specifically, fossils of ancient relatives of living chimpanzees. They could show which traits chimpanzees inherited from our common ancestor and which they acquired after their lineage branched off. Unfortunately, the fossil record of chimpanzees is wretched. In fact, it has yet to be discovered. Gorillas are just as

# The Chimpanzee Genome Project

The sequencing of the human genome, completed in 2003, was a grand achievement for biology. But it didn't take long for the same sequencing labs that had cracked our own code to turn their technology on another species: the chimpanzee. Why were these researchers so eager to start work on the chimp genome? Because it will help them make sense of our own genetic code, and understand how it evolved.

Scientists have been making comparisons between human and chimpanzee genes for years, but before the age of genomes the work was slow and the yields minor. It could take months to decode the sequence of just a fragment of a single gene. Still, the results of these early comparisons were surprising: chimpanzees and humans showed striking similarities on the genetic level. Scientists estimated that chimpanzee and human DNA were 98 to 99 percent identical. This similarity has helped reveal chimpanzees as our closest living relatives. We share a common ancestor that lived just a few million years ago. Only after the human and chimpanzee lineages split did each one evolve the differences that distinguish them today.

Now, with the Chimpanzee Genome Project moving quickly forward, our understanding of the similarities and differences between our two species is moving forward as well. In 2004, Japanese researchers published the first fine-scale comparison of an entire chromosome. In humans this chromosome is known as chromosome 21; the equivalent in chimpanzees is chromosome 22. The researchers sorted the differences between the chromosomes into the different kinds of mutations that caused them. In some cases, a single letter in the genetic code was altered. The researchers found that 1.44 percent of the chromosomes differed in this way. But they found other changes that previous studies had missed. At thousands of spots in each chromosome, a stretch of DNA hundreds or thousands of letters long had been snipped out. In other places, the reverse had occurred: a stretch of DNA had been accidentally duplicated and then inserted into another part of the genome.

These mutations mark off our species from other primates. Many of them may have had no real effect on us; they may have struck regions of the genome that do not contain genes, for example. On the other hand, other mutations have produced profound changes. One of the first genes in which scientists found significant signs of evolution is known as FOXP2. It shows signs of having evolved rapidly less than 200,000 years ago. As we'll see in Chapter 6, its evolution may have played a key role in the rise of human language. Pinpointing the genes that make us uniquely human will also help medical researchers.

Why is it, for example, that chimpanzees don't get AIDS or Alzheimer's, despite their similar genetic make-up? Their genome may hold clues.

Of course, there is no single chimpanzee genome, just as there is no single human genome. Each individual chimpanzee has a unique genetic code. A full understanding of the workings of chimpanzee DNA—and thus our own—will only be possible if scientists can gather chimp genomes from many populations. They will also need to compare what they observe in chimp DNA to what primatologists see in the wild—how chimpanzees behave, how they resist diseases, and so on.

Chimpanzees and humans have strikingly similar DNA. The differences between them may hold clues to how we evolved.

Tragically, though, just as we humans are getting to know our cousins, we are also pushing them toward extinction. Deforestation, hunting and human-triggered epidemics of anthrax and other diseases are wiping out chimpanzees at a rapid rate. If wild chimps disappear, it will be a disaster not only for the world's biodiversity but also for our knowledge of ourselves.

bad. For millions of years these apes have lived in rain forests, where fossils tend not to form, and the fossils that do form are not exposed on bare rock faces but are buried under wet soil. The poor quality of the ape fossil record extends even farther back in time. Scientists have found hardly any African ape fossils from the time period between seven million and thirteen million years ago.

Historically, scientists have been less interested in finding fossil chimps or apes than in finding fossil hominids. The first real glimpse paleoanthropologists had of ancient hominids came in the 1890s, when Eugene Dubois unearthed a slope-browed skull in Indonesia. Today, Java Man (as it was subsequently dubbed) is recognized as a 900,000-year-old member of the species *Homo erectus*.

It would take another thirty years for someone to find an older hominid. In 1924, a young South African anatomist named Raymond Dart was given a collection of primate skulls that had been dug up in a quarry. One of the skulls, Dart realized, was actually a young member of our own lineage. He noted, for example, that the skull was positioned directly over its spine, a trait found in humans but not in other apes. This skull became known as the

Seven skulls of ancient relatives of living humans. From left to right: *Adapis* (50 million years ago), *Proconsul* (23 to 15 million years ago), *Australopithecus africanus* (3.5 to 2.5 million years ago), *Homo habilis* (2.3 to 1.7 million years ago), *Homo erectus* (1.8 million years ago to 30,000 years ago), *Homo sapiens* (a 92,000-year-old skull from Israel) and *Homo sapiens* (a 22,000-year-old skull from France).

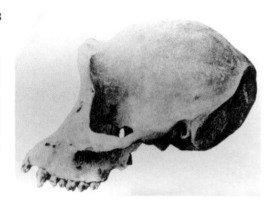

Eugene Dubois made this drawing of Java Man, a *Homo erectus* fossil he discovered in Indonesia in 1891.

Taung Child. It is now recognized as a member of the hominid species *Australopithecus africanus*, dating back roughly 2.4 million years.

Over the next few decades, a handful of new hominid species emerged. Except for *Homo erectus*, which was found in China as well as Indonesia, these species were all discovered in Africa. Or rather, one part of Africa: the Rift Valley, running from South Africa to Ethiopia. Over time, paleoanthropologists came to see this region as the cradle of hominid evolution.

In 1973, paleoanthropologist Donald Johanson and his colleagues discovered the first of a series of remarkable hominid fossils at the north end of the rift, in Ethiopia. They excavated 40 percent of a 3.2-million-year-old female—a find that was downright spectacular in a field where scientists can get excited by a single tooth. The researchers named her Lucy, after the Beatles song that was playing in the camp around the time of the discovery: "Lucy in the Sky With Diamonds." The researchers soon found other fossils from the same species, which they dubbed *Australopithecus afarensis*. It displayed an unprecedented mix of human and ape-like traits. *Australopithecus afarensis* was small—Lucy probably stood only about three and a half feet high and weighed seventy pounds. Its chest had a chimp-like funnel shape, rather than the barrel shape of humans. It had long arms and hooked fingers. *Australopithecus afarensis* also had a small brain—a large male's brain might reach 450 cubic centimeters, one-third the size of a human's. But Lucy also had many traits found today only in humans and not in other apes—most importantly its upright, biped anatomy (a subject we'll explore in the next chapter).

During the rest of the 1970s and 1980s, paleoanthropologists discovered new hominid fossils, but none older than Lucy. It was not until 1994 that Tim White, of the University of California at Berkeley (a one-time coworker with Johanson on Lucy), pushed the hominid record back in time. Digging in Ethiopia with Gen Suwa and Berhane Asfaw, he discovered fossils of a new species, which the scientists named *Ardipithecus ramidus*. The fossils dated back 4.4 million years, a full million years older than Lucy. Over the course of the next decade, paleoanthropologists discovered still more pre-Lucy hominids, culminating (for the moment, at any rate) with *Sahelanthropus*. Dating back somewhere between six and seven million years old, *Sahelanthropus* is roughly twice as old as Lucy.

Paleoanthropologists are now trying to figure out what all of these fossils tell us about our evolutionary tree. It may have been bushy at its base, or something closer to a straight trunk. The advocates of a bushy base argue

A large portion of the skeleton of Lucy. This individual belonged to the species *Australopithecus afarensis*, which existed from three to two million years ago.

that early hominids don't fit along a simple progression from ape-like to human-like forms. For example, although the skull of *Sahelanthropus* looks a lot like a chimp from the back, it has small canine tooth crowns, which have only been discovered on much more recent hominid species. These scientists argue that the variation found in early hominids hints that there is a huge diversity of other species from the same age waiting to be discovered.

But many paleoanthropologists aren't convinced that our tree is quite so bushy. Tim White points out that a single species of any mammal can contain very different-looking individuals. He argues that many hominid fossils have wrongly been assigned to species of their own, when in fact they should be lumped together. The three oldest known hominids—each known from only a few bones—are currently considered to be three different species: *Sahelanthropus tchadensis*, *Orrorin tugensis* and *Ardipithecus kadabba* (a 5.7-million-year-old precursor of *Ardipithecus ramidus*). But White and his colleagues have compared the teeth of these hominids and have suggested that they may all actually belong to the same species.

While much remains uncertain about the early days of our evolution, one thing is certain: *Sahelanthropus* will not be the last word on hominid origins. Fossils dating back to the same age, or even older, will eventually rise from their hiding places in the Earth. But it may not be easy to tell exactly where they fit on the hominid tree. In some cases, scientists may well discover apes that have evolved a few supposedly unique hominid traits on their own. In other cases, the earliest hominids may still share so many primitive traits with other apes that it may be hard to tell they are hominids at all. Certainly the discovery of even older hominid fossils will be greeted with applause and headlines. But it will inspire some head-scratching as well.

This tree shows the evolution of the hominid species described in this book. The red lines mark the age range of fossils known for each species. The green lines represent current hypotheses about how these species evolved from common ancestors. The boxes show the four major groups of hominid species recognized by most paleoanthropologists. Paleoanthropologists are divided over how early hominids gave rise to the later groups. The thick branches connecting the boxes show the basic consensus about how the groups are related.

# EVOLUTIONARY TREE

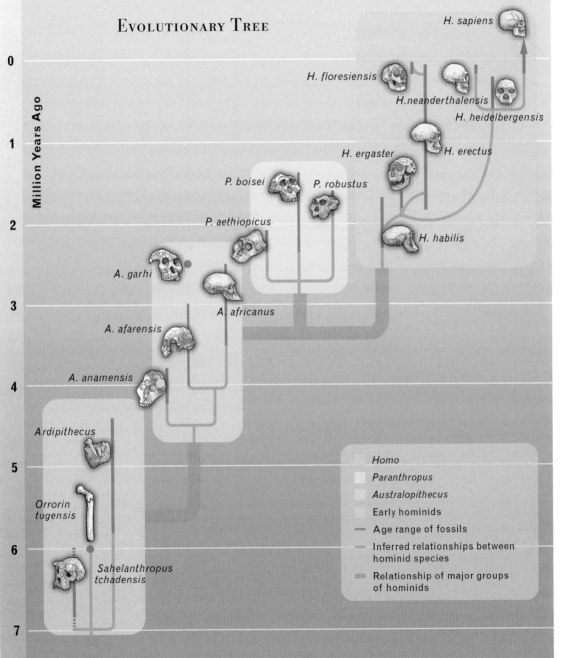

**Million Years Ago**

H. sapiens

H. floresiensis

H.neanderthalensis

H. heidelbergensis

H. ergaster

H. erectus

P. boisei

P. robustus

P. aethiopicus

H. habilis

A. garhi

A. africanus

A. afarensis

A. anamensis

Ardipithecus

Orrorin tugensis

Sahelanthropus tchadensis

Homo

Paranthropus

Australopithecus

Early hominids

— Age range of fossils

— Inferred relationships between hominid species

Relationship of major groups of hominids

# Myth of the Missing Link

When the discovery of *Sahelanthropus* was announced in 2002, *The Christian Science Monitor* declared that the fossil might well be "the holy grail of anthropology: the missing link between humans and their ape forebears." Newspapers love to use the phrase "missing link," because it's what most people think the science of evolution is all about. But in fact it's not. The missing link is a myth that has sowed confusion for more than 130 years.

When Darwin published *The Descent of Man* in 1871, many readers mistakenly thought that he was arguing that humans descended from living apes such as chimpanzees and gorillas. Darwin's opponents argued that, despite the minor similarities between humans and apes, the gulf between them was too great to span with a chain of intermediate forms. What's more, there was no evidence in the fossil record of a so-called "missing link"—an ancestor of living humans that connected our species to living apes.

Reviewing *The Descent of Man*, a writer for the *London Times* expressed a common sort of disbelief: "It is almost incredible that no evidence should be producible of the existence of apelike creatures," he wrote. "We have the undoubted and recorded experience of at least four thousand years of history ... during which many races have been subjected to influences the most diversified and the most favorable to the further development

of their faculties ... [yet] the earliest known examples of Man's most essential characteristics exhibit his faculties in the greatest perfection ever attained. No poetry surpasses Homer."

In the 1890s, the Dutch doctor Eugene Dubois went to Indonesia and discovered fossils of a creature that seemed to fit the popular notion of a missing link. The so-called Java Man had human-like proportions, but it also had intermediate traits, such as a braincase that was smaller than a human's but larger than an ape's. However, *Homo erectus* also had a huge brow ridge and other puzzling features that couldn't be found on either living apes or living humans. It thus didn't fit the notion of a missing link, and so Dubois's critics suggested that it was actually a mélange of different species—part gibbon, part Neanderthal, part sickly human. Today paleontologists recognize that Dubois had in fact discovered an extinct hominid: *Homo erectus*, which existed from 1.8 million years ago to less than 100,000 years ago.

While Java Man revealed a great deal about our ancestry, it doesn't fit the popular conception of a missing link. That's because this notion has no place in Darwin's theory of evolution. Darwin never argued that living apes gave rise to some species that then gave rise to humans. Instead, he proposed that living apes and humans shared a common ancestor, as did many extinct species.

Today, with some twenty species of hominids

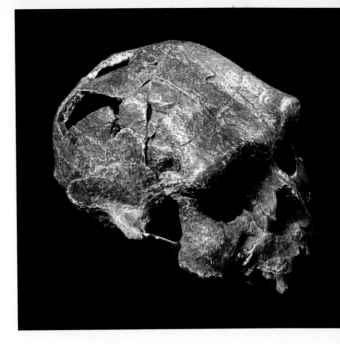

*Homo erectus* became extinct perhaps only 30,000 years ago. It represents a separate branch of hominid evolution, not a "missing link."

discovered, it's easier to see how misleading the notion of a missing link can be. There's a healthy debate about some of the relationships between these species. But their relationships are probably close to the ones shown in the tree on page 41.

Our own species may trace a direct line of ancestry to *Homo erectus*. But *Homo erectus* survived for over a million years after that split. The Asian branch of *Homo erectus*—to which Dubois's Java Man belonged—had little or nothing to do with our ancestry. Those hominids acquired some peculiar features of their own, such as strongly ridged cranium walls, that we humans did not inherit. Java Man was almost certainly our cousin, not our grandfather. The same probably goes for *Sahelanthropus*. It branched off much closer to the base of the hominid tree, but it is not a missing link either, no matter what newspapers may shout. Instead, it has a mix of anatomy, some of which is unique to its own lineage and not to our own.

What about the species that was the common ancestor of humans and chimpanzees? Couldn't that be considered the missing link? No, because the only reason it is significant to us is because chimpanzees and bonobos are our closest *living* relatives. Just imagine that in fifty years chimpanzees and bonobos become extinct (a scenario that sadly isn't that far from reality). Gorillas would then take the title of our closest living relatives. That would mean that the missing link would no longer be the common ancestor we share with chimpanzees, but the older one we share with gorillas.

The term "missing link" serves no good purpose today. Creationists use it to try to cast doubt on the reality of evolution whenever a new hominid fossil is discovered. They point out the features of the fossil that aren't shared by humans or living apes, and claim that those traits are proof that the hominid couldn't have bridged the two groups. These arguments hardly call human evolution into doubt. The only lesson that should be drawn from them is that the term "missing link" should be retired for good.

## CHAPTER THREE

# THE WALK BEGINS

When Darwin set out to put humans in his evolutionary zoo, his challenge was clear: to take all of the qualities that seemed unique to mankind, that seemed to set us fundamentally apart from other animals, and to figure out how they might have gradually evolved. He contemplated how natural selection might have produced language. He pondered the evolution of toolmaking. He even dared to consider the biological roots of morality. But before all other changes, Darwin realized, came the most obvious. He had to get *Homo sapiens* up on two feet.

"Man alone has become a biped," he declared in *The Descent of Man*, "and we can, I think, partly see how he has come to assume his erect attitude, which forms one of his most conspicuous characters."

To say that man had *become* a biped was an audacious statement in Darwin's time. Man, most naturalists agreed, was designed as a biped because that design suited his place in the natural order. Fish swam in the sea, earthworms slithered through the soil, horses walked on all fours. But man alone stood tall. Our stance allowed us to look up to heaven above and freed our hands to serve our will. For evidence of this design, the theologian William Paley pointed out how hard it is simply to stand. "It is more remarkable in two-legged animals than in quadrupeds, and, most of all, as being the tallest, and resting upon the smallest

*Australopithecus anamensis* lived about four million years ago in Kenya. Anatomical details suggest that it might have walked upright.

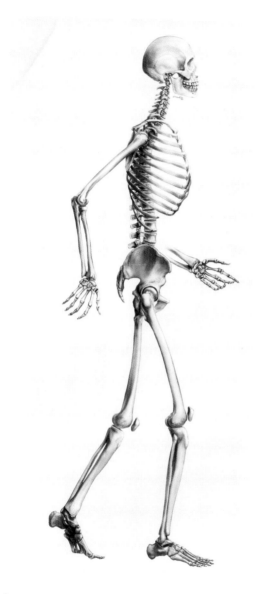

The human skeleton has many adaptations for standing and moving bipedally, such as long legs and short, stiff feet.

base, in man," he wrote in his 1802 book, *Natural Theology*. Ankle bones, knee joints, spine, hips and legs all have to work together to keep the human tower upright. If any part fails, we tumble in a heap.

Darwin began to see our upright stance in a different light. He envisioned ground-walking humans having evolved from tree-dwelling apes. Our arboreal ancestors might have used their hands to grab things such as branches, nuts and insects, just as living monkeys and apes do today. "With their fingers they pull out thorns and burrs, and hunt for each other's parasites," Darwin observed. "They roll down stones, or throw them at their enemies: nevertheless, they are clumsy in these various actions, and, as I have myself seen, are quite unable to throw a stone with precision."

Natural selection might favor monkeys with hands that allowed them to throw stones or grab insects more skillfully. But any adaptation for these sorts of movements might make a monkey clumsier in the trees. How did our own ancestors escape the trade-off that traps monkeys? By coming down to the ground, Darwin argued. Our ancestors began to walk on two legs, and in the process their hands became free to evolve. As our ancestors spent more time walking, their feet evolved as well. Instead of long, grasping toes, flat feet were favored. The spine curved and the pelvis became broader, to support the upper body.

"If it be an advantage to man to stand firmly on his feet," Darwin wrote, "and to have his hands and arms free, of which, from his pre-eminent success in the battle of life, there can be no doubt, then I can see no reason why it should not have been advantageous to the progenitors of man to have become more and more erect or bipedal."

Experts today agree that Darwin's basic idea was both brilliant and sound. All their evidence supports the hypothesis that our ancestors evolved from quadrupeds into bipeds. But researchers today have also exposed some serious flaws in Darwin's hypothesis. He offered no explanation for why natural selection led our ancestors to move down from the trees in the first place. And once they came down, Darwin did not offer an explanation for why they became bipedal. One does not inevitably lead to the other. Other primates, such as baboons, came down from the trees and adapted to the ground as well, but they still walk on all fours. But the biggest of the flaws in Darwin's hypothesis would not become apparent for over a century. Darwin saw bipedalism as inextricably linked with a whole-scale transformation of our ancestors, from their hands to their brains. It turns out that our ancestors became bipedal apes millions of years before they acquired other distinctly human traits.

Darwin could not have known any of this, because the first fossils of early hominids were discovered over thirty years after his death. When paleontologists did finally find them, it was no simple matter to tell whether they were bipeds. In 1924 Raymond Dart discovered the skull of an *Australopithecus africanus* child. He could not look at its feet to see if they were flat or curved, or at its hips to see if they were narrow or broad. But Dart, a brilliant neuroanatomist, knew how to

extract clues from a skull that others might miss. Like all primates, the Taung Child had a hole at the base of its skull where its spinal cord exited. The hole (known as the foramen magnum) was located toward the center of the skull, as it is in humans. In chimpanzees and other apes, it is located toward the rear. The hole's location, Dart argued, reflects how each species stands. In humans, the skull sits on top of the erect spine. In chimpanzees, the spine slopes away. The *A. africanus* child, Dart concluded, stood like a human.

If Dart was right, hominids were upright at least 2.4 million years ago. Later discoveries pushed bipedality back millions of years more. In 1978, Maeve Leakey and her colleagues discovered hominid footprints in 3.5-million-year-old volcanic ash at Laetoli, Tanzania. The impressions showed that the creatures who made them—probably members of Lucy's species, *A. afarensis*—were standing on two feet as they walked.

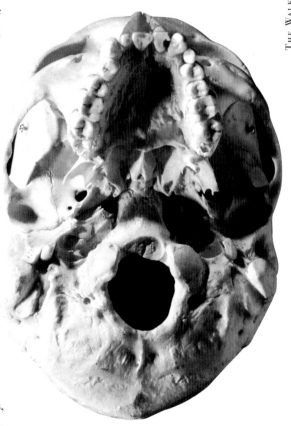

A human skull shown from the underside, with its lower jaw removed. The large round hole is the foramen magnum.

Taung Child, an *Australopithecus africanus* skull, offered some of the first clues that extinct hominids stood upright. As in humans, the hole for its spinal cord is situated at the base of the skull.

Above: A reconstruction of Lucy
(*Australopithecus afarensis*).
Opposite: Paleoanthropologists suspect *A. afarensis* left bipedal footprints at Laetoli, Tanzania, some 3.5 million years ago.

In the thirty years since the discovery of these footprints, the evidence for bipedality has reached nearly three million years farther back in hominid evolution. French and English researchers discovered the bones of *Orrorin tugensis*, a six-million-year-old hominid, in Kenya in 2002. One of the bones they found was the ball joint at the top of *Orrorin*'s femur, which would have buttressed the femur against its hip. The connection between the ball joint and the femur itself is similar to later, upright hominids. It suggests that the ball joint was bearing all of the weight of *Orrorin*'s upper body, as ours does. *Sahelanthropus*, which is estimated to be between six and seven million years old, is known so far only from skull fragments, but even these fossils have yielded hints of upright walking. The hole at its base, the foramen magnum, is under the center of the skull, as in humans, and not near the rear, as in knuckle-walking apes.

In other words, as far back as paleoanthropologists can look, our hominid ancestors seem to have been at least partially bipedal. Walking upright may have been the first major transformation that set off hominids from other apes. But as far as paleoanthropologists can tell, standing upright did not immediately trigger a revolution of the sort that Darwin proposed. The oldest stone tools yet found are only 2.6 million years old. Hominid brains didn't get significantly larger than

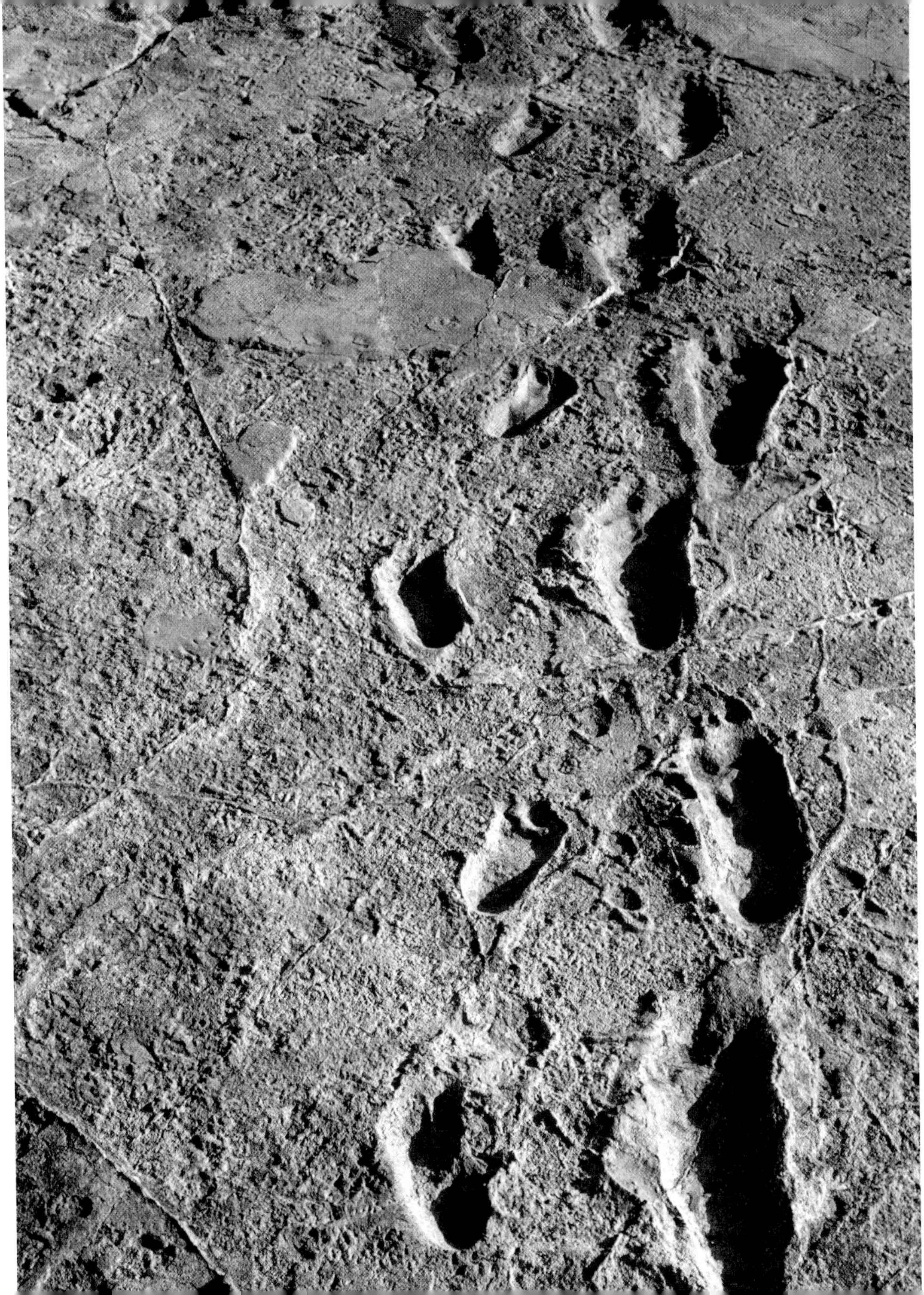

a chimpanzee's until about two million years ago. In other words, for over half of hominid history, they were basically bipedal apes.

At the same time, the discovery of ancient walkers has challenged some traditional explanations about how our ancestors came down from the trees. For decades, many researchers believed the move was driven by the rise of the African savanna. The vast tropical forests spanning much of Africa disintegrated, with eastern and southern Africa turning to dry grasslands. The ancestors of gorillas and chimpanzees found refuge in the forests of central and western Africa. But our ancestors happened to live where savannas took over, and adapted to the new habitat. They began walking bipedally to cover the long distances from one patch of trees to the next. Standing upright might also let them see farther across the open plains, to spot distant trees or oncoming leopards.

Paleoecologists have painstakingly reconstructed African ecosystems, tracking the changes that have taken place over the past twenty million years. They have dug up fossil pollen spores and analyzed the chemistry of ancient soil. They have found that grasslands did indeed replace woodlands in many regions of Africa—probably in part because of the continuing drop in carbon dioxide levels, which produced a cooler, drier climate. But the timing of the change doesn't fit traditional accounts of bipedalism. Hominids did not live in full-blown savannas until about two million years ago. The oldest hominids appear to have lived in a

The Olduvai Gorge in Tanzania has yielded a wealth of hominid fossils that have helped shed light on the evolution of bipedalism.

Chimpanzees can walk bipedally, although they do so only rarely.

mix of forests and open woodlands. It was in this environment, not in open grass-lands, where our ancestors became upright.

Now scientists are looking for clues of the evolutionary pressure that led hominids to become bipedal in the forest. To do so, they must figure out what upright walking evolved from. Some scientists believe that chimpanzees, gorillas and humans all share a knuckle-walking ancestor. They claim that many features in the wrists of humans and extinct hominids show signs of this ancestry. If that's true, then chimpanzees may indeed offer some clues. Craig Stanford of the University of California, who has observed chimpanzees in the wild for years, has witnessed them stand up and even walk bipedally on rare occasions. Chimpanzees that climb into trees sometimes stand upright in order to pluck a fig just overhead. When they're on the ground, they may stand up to pull a low-hanging branch to get at its fruit.

Grabbing overhead food may have driven our ancestors onto their feet, Stanford suggests, because their food was becoming more unpredictable. Climate change caused densely packed stands of fruit trees to become scattered through open woodlands. Thickets grew in patches rather than carpets. In earlier years a steady supply of rain allowed the plants to produce a constant supply of fruits and seeds. But now rains came more seasonally, and so plants produced food more seasonally as well. Stanford suggests that hominids may have begun to stand up in order to pluck fruit on low-hanging branches. Gradually they began to move longer distances to find other trees.

Scientists are finding ways to test hypotheses for the evolution of upright walking. Some have measured how much energy humans use walking upright and chimpanzees use walking on their knuckles. It turns out that bipedal walking demands significantly less energy, which supports the idea that a demand for efficiency was an important element in hominid evolution. Meanwhile, Elaine Videan and William McGrew at Miami University in Ohio tested chimpanzees at the Cincinnati Zoo to see what sort of conditions prompt them to walk bipedally. For example, they put piles of bananas and other fruit in the chimp enclosures to see if the apes would walk upright in order to carry armfuls of fruit to their favorite eating spots. Videan and McGrew found that the chimpanzees did walk upright more often in order to carry food. Likewise, putting the food on platforms prompted the chimpanzees to stand up more on two legs. On the other hand, putting up barriers to block their view didn't encourage them to become more upright. Videan and McGrew's results are consistent with the notion that foraging and gathering played an important role in getting our ancestors on their feet.

Yet these comparisons can go only so far, because chimpanzees are not automatic stand-ins for our ancestors. Nothing can take the place of fossils, and unfortunately many of the oldest hominids are known from little more than their skulls. The oldest relatively complete skeletons belong to younger species, such as Lucy and her fellow *Australopithecus afarensis*, which lived three million to four million years ago. And even these skeletons leave plenty of room for debate.

The first studies on *Australopithecus afarensis* were carried out by Owen Lovejoy of Kent State University in Ohio and his colleagues. They found that its hip and femur fit together so as to allow it to make a full, striding gait much like modern humans. But other researchers, such as Randall Susman at the State University of New York, saw other traits in *A. afarensis*'s skeleton suggesting that it still spent a lot of time in the trees. Its arms were long relative to its legs, for example, and its fingers and toes were curved—all of which might have been adaptations for gripping branches. Moreover, Lucy had a shoulder joint that was tilted more toward its head than a human shoulder, which might help it swing its arms more as it climbed. Susman and others even questioned how well Lucy could walk on the ground with her relatively short legs. They

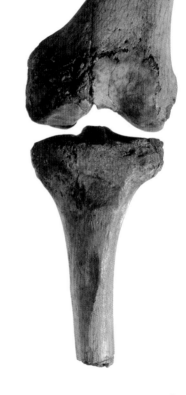

The knee joint of *Australopithecus afarensis* is one of many anatomical details scientists have studied to determine how it walked.

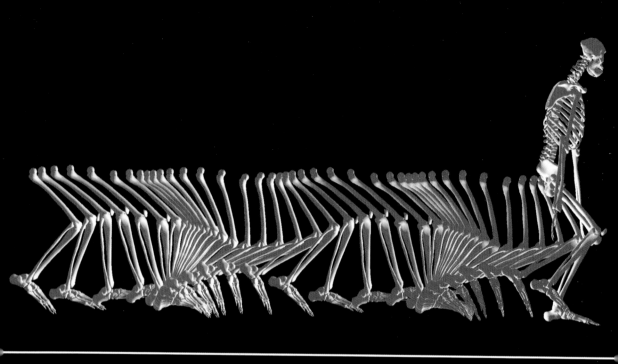
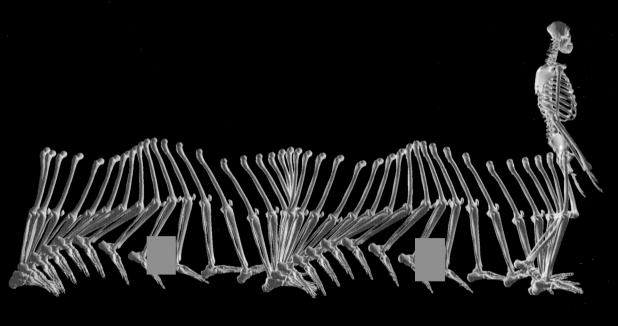

envisioned her and her fellow *A. afarensis* bent at the hips and never straightening their legs as they walked, a bit like Groucho Marx. Some have even suggested that Lucy walked on her knuckles.

Given *A. afarensis*'s place on the hominid evolutionary tree, it isn't terribly surprising that Lucy's bones are like a chimp in some ways and like a human in others. But that insight doesn't show how her anatomical mosaic worked in real life. In recent years, scientists have pioneered a promising way out of this dilemma: making Lucy walk. They have created three-dimensional reconstructions of Lucy's skeleton in computers, and then calculated how much energy a hominid would need to use to walk either like Groucho Marx or upright. Research at the University of Liverpool suggests that walking like Groucho Marx would have put such a strain on Lucy's body that she would have quickly overheated. Similar work at Arizona State University also found that Lucy would prefer an upright gait. But with her short legs, she could only manage a speed of about a mile an hour. And her hips, which were broader than those of humans, swiveled forward with each stride. But nevertheless, she held herself relatively upright.

While many mysteries about the evolution of bipedalism remain, it is clear that it was not abrupt. Although early hominids may have been able to walk upright, three million years later Lucy was still awkward on the ground compared to our own species. Over a million more years would pass before efficient long-distance walkers evolved. We're not ready yet to meet these hominids, though. First we must trace two other major threads of hominid evolution: our technology and our brains.

Scientists are using computers to see how easily hominids could walk in different stances. These images come from a study at the University of Liverpool of *Australopithecus afarensis* walking with bent knees (top) and in a more upright stance (bottom).

# Orangutans: Walkers in the Air?

Most scientists who want to understand how our ancestors evolved into bipedal walkers look to the ground. Robin Crompton, an expert on locomotion at the University of Liverpool, believes they're looking in the wrong place. He thinks that the first crucial steps toward bipedality took place up in the trees.

Scientists have been attracted to the hypothesis that we descend from knuckle-walking apes because—among other reasons—our closest living relatives walk that way. Gorillas, bonobos and chimpanzees all spend much of their time walking on the ground, and they all knuckle-walk to get from place to place. It's reasonable to suggest that all of these apes descended from ancestors that left the trees around eight million years ago and took on a knuckle-walking way of life. In support of this hypothesis, some researchers have pointed to the fact that gorillas, chimpanzees, bonobos and humans all share a peculiar foot. When all four species walk, their feet make contact with the ground from heel to toe. (Most mammals only use their toes to walk.) Presumably this special adaptation—and many others—evolved as our common ancestor adapted to life on the ground.

Crompton and his colleagues have cast doubt on this line of reasoning by showing that orangutans can also walk with a full-foot stride. They had a captive orangutan walk over a force-sensitive plate and found that its stride was surprisingly similar to that of humans—much more so than other apes.

What's even more tantalizing to Crompton is the fact that orangutans also use the same stride to move through trees. They walk on a branch, while using their arms to grab overhanging

This 1875 illustration compares the skeletons of a gorilla and a human. Gorillas lean on their knuckles as they walk, while humans stay upright.

branches or vines to steady their motion. This sort of movement sets orangutans apart from monkeys, which travel through trees typically with their backs held horizontally, using their hands and feet to grasp the same branch.

Crompton argues that we have to look much farther in the past to find the origins of human bipedality, to the common ancestor of all great apes, including orangutans. According to current research on primate DNA, this ancient ape must have lived twelve to fifteen million years ago. Crompton proposes that large-bodied apes evolved adaptations in their muscles and skeleton for bipedal movement while they still lived in the trees. The ancestors of gorillas and chimpanzees, he suggests, moved down to the ground and became knuckle-walkers

only after their lineages branched off from other apes. That means that the first hominids still lived in the trees some six to seven million years ago. When they came down, they adapted to the ground not by walking on their knuckles, but by walking upright.

If Crompton is right, some of the big dilemmas of human evolution might disappear. Scientists have been puzzled, for example, by the anatomy of hominids such as Lucy (*Australopithecus afarensis*). They had long arms and hook-like fingers, which seem like adaptations to tree-climbing. But they could also move relatively efficiently on the ground by walking upright. Some researchers have called this mix of traits a mysterious mosaic. But Crompton argues that it's exactly what you'd expect if hominids descended from orangutan-like ancestors who first walked through the trees.

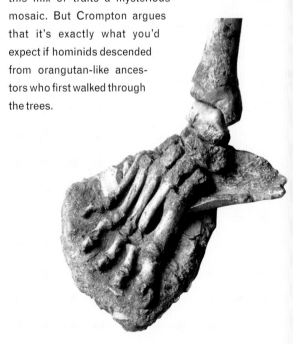

The foot of a Neanderthal is adapted for walking bipedally — on the ground, not in the trees.

# THE TOOLMAKERS

In northeast Ethiopia, the Gona River flows through dry, rugged hills. There is no shortage of rocks to be found there: some flat, some round, some half buried, some sitting on the surface. To most people, these rocks look pretty much alike. But in the 1970s, a team of paleoanthropologists noticed that some of them were peculiar. They had edges and facets that ordinary geology could not produce. Instead, these rocks had been shaped by hand and transformed into tools. In the late 1980s, the researchers—led by Sileshi Semaw, then at Rutgers University—began to look systematically for these tools and for layers of volcanic ash that might provide an age for them. The age they calculated was staggeringly old: almost 2.6 million years ago. These stones are the oldest hominid tools yet discovered.

Tools help define us as a species. We may not be the only species to make them, but no other species makes them as well as we do, or depends on them as much. Just try to imagine how miserable our existence would be without tools—finding food with our bare hands and then not being able to cook or chop it before eating it, and finding shelter only in a tree or a cave. Our reliance is so profound that our tools have even altered our bodies. The areas of our brains responsible for using tools, such as the regions that control our

For most of hominid evolution, technological change was extremely slow.
Left: a 1.7- million-year-old pebble tool.
Right: a 1-million-year-old hand axe.

hands, are enlarged compared with other primates. Our hands are different, allowing us to touch our fingertips together. A number of paleoanthropologists argue that toolmaking allowed our ancestors to occupy a new ecological niche. With tools, hominids could find food in places that were previously off-limits. And that food supply may have helped fuel bigger, more powerful brains and helped give hominids longer lifespans. Tools would ultimately allow humans to alter the world, to survive in almost any climate and to let them explore other planets.

Every great discovery in evolution raises as many questions as it answers, and the tools of Gona are no exception. Why did hominids start making stone tools 2.6 million years ago? Did earlier hominids make tools out of wood or leaves or some other material that didn't fossilize? Just how far back do we have to go in our history to find the earliest roots of tool use?

No one knows the answers to these questions, but a number of primatologists argue that they will be found in the distant past—millions of years before the first hominids walked through the African woodlands. They base their claim on the fact that humans are not the only primates that make and use tools. Orangutans, for example, use branches to ward off bees or wasps. They dip leaves into deep holes to drink water, and strip twigs in order to stick them into ant nests or spiny fruits. Chimpanzees make insect probes as well. They also place nuts on flat rocks and smash them with pebbles. They sometimes lay out several leaves on wet ground to keep their backsides dry.

The fact that humans, chimpanzees and orangutans all make tools doesn't necessarily mean that the common ancestor of all the great apes was making tools twelve million years ago. For one thing, gorillas have never been observed making tools. For another, you can find toolmakers beyond the great apes. Crows on the Pacific island of New Caledonia, for example, can fashion a

Hominids probably used these 1.8-million-year-old stone tools to butcher carcasses and obtain other sorts of food.

twig into a hook, which they then hold in their beak in order to fish for insect larvae. No one would argue from their skill that the common ancestor of crows and humans (a 350-million-year-old lizard-like creature) used tools as well.

It's possible that the ancestor of the great apes was instead "preadapted" for making tools, rather than a toolmaker itself. Richard Byrne, a primatologist at the University of St. Andrews in Scotland, has pointed out that great apes are unusual as primates go for their ability to extract hard-to-eat foods. Gorillas, for example, can enjoy a meal of stinging nettles because they can remove the tiny spines from the plants. Chimpanzees in Tanzania feed on the hard-to-eat fruits of the vine *Saba florida*. The chimps first have to free a fruit from a vine, break open its hard shell to expose its interior, divide it into smaller sections to eat, remove the pieces of shell still attached to the sections and, finally, extract the sweet flesh inside.

Chimpanzee hands have different proportions from humans, which may make it difficult for them to craft stone tools.

This sort of diet requires two traits: nimble fingers and a brain capable of long-term planning. At many stages in eating *Saba* fruits, a chimpanzee's two hands are doing different jobs, and sometimes it may dedicate individual fingers to different tasks. The chimpanzee has to choose at every step from several possible actions,

Left: Chimpanzees often use tools, such as these leaves, which can act like a sponge for soaking up water.

depending on the size of the fruit, the thickness of the shell and so on. Not only does the chimpanzee have to handle each immediate challenge, but it also has to bear in mind how they all fit into its long-term goal of lunch.

Both nimble fingers and a planning brain might have been preadaptations for making tools. When chimpanzees want to crack open nuts with rocks, they may pick out the perfect hammer-shaped stone and carry it a quarter of a mile before they reach their favorite nut-cracking site. To make a termite-fishing probe, they may break off the end of a stick and strip off small branches so that it can fit in a nest hole.

Ape brains may have also evolved in response to a different force: their complicated social lives. Robin Dunbar, a University of Liverpool psychologist, has argued that this complexity makes special demands on a primate brain. With more friends and enemies to keep track of, primates need more processing power.

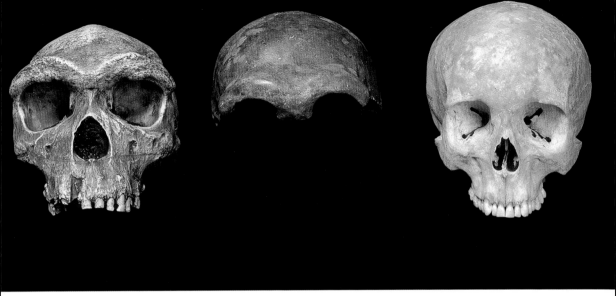

Dunbar hypothesized that in primate species that form big groups, natural selection should favor big, powerful brains. To see if he was right, Dunbar compared the average group size of primates with the dimensions of their brain. In particular, he looked at the neocortex, the outer layer of the brain that is responsible for

From left to right: *Australopithecus africanus, Homo rudolfensis, Homo erectus, Homo heidelbergensis, Homo neanderthalensis* and *Homo sapiens*. More recent hominids have larger skulls than earlier species, reflecting the evolution of a larger brain.

the most sophisticated, abstract thought. He found that the relative size of the neocortex increases with the average group size, just as he had predicted. In particular, he found that some apes have the biggest groups and the biggest neocortices of all primates except for humans.

A bigger brain may have not only helped primates cope with their social world but might have also helped provide the mental powers required to make tools. And the social lives of apes may have also encouraged tool use in another way: by providing an opportunity for young apes to learn from old ones. Apes, after all, don't have an innate instinct to make termite sticks or bee swatters. They must learn how to do these things, and watching more experienced apes helps novice apes learn faster. It can take years for a young chimpanzee to learn how to crack nuts with a rock with real skill.

Does this mean that our ancestors had a cultural tradition of tool-making ten million years ago? It's a hard question to answer with fossils. The sticks and leaves crafted by living apes rot away quickly. Chimpanzees use rocks as hammers and anvils to crack nuts but, unlike hominid stone tools, they don't look noticeably different from ordinary rocks. On the other hand, chimpanzees do tend to create piles of rocks in certain places where they like to crack nuts. Perhaps some day a smart paleontologist will recognize one of these nut-cracking sites dating back eight million years.

For now, however, we can't know how far back our toolmaking tradition reaches. Early hominids may well have used sticks to probe for nuts, and stones to smash insects—or not. Only at Gona does speculation give way—at least a little— to hard evidence.

Sileshi Semaw and his colleagues have found that in order to make their tools, hominids at Gona traveled to the bank of a river to collect rounded cobbles, which they then carried away into the flood plains. There, they knocked off pieces of the cobbles to create cutting edges. Semaw and his colleagues have also found bones of large grazing mammals at these sites, with distinctive cut marks that could not have been made by teeth. Instead, they bear the hallmarks of having been made with sharp stone tools. The hominids of Gona were most likely slicing meat off carcasses in order to eat it. No hominid fossils have been found yet alongside these tools and cut bones. But not far away, in 2.5-million-year-old rocks, researchers have found fossils of a hominid known as *Australopithecus garhi* alongside mammal bones with similar cut marks.

While researchers have only found pieces of *A. garhi*'s skull, the discovery is enough to pose a fascinating puzzle. *A. garhi*'s brain was 450 cubic centimeters, only slightly bigger than a chimpanzee's. Does that mean that hominids 2.6 million years ago had fundamentally chimp-like mental powers? If that were true, it might mean that living chimpanzees can learn how to make tools.

To test this possibility, Nicholas Toth of Indiana University tried to teach a very bright bonobo named Kanzi to make hominid-quality stone tools. He and his colleagues put some food in a box, which they secured with a string. In order to get at the food, Kanzi had to cut the string. In order to cut the string, he had to put a cutting edge on a rock by smashing another rock against it. Toth demonstrated how to do this many times, and Kanzi did his best to imitate his teacher.

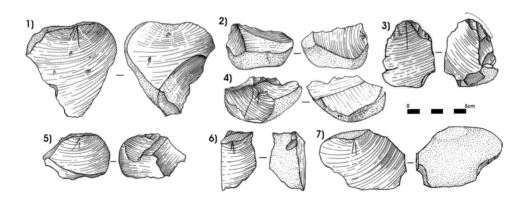

The oldest known stone tools, found in Gona, Ethiopia, date back 2.6 million years. Each of these seven drawings shows the front and back of a tool. Hominids made the tools by hitting one rock with another, knocking off flakes. Both the flakes and the remaining cores were used, probably for cutting meat from carcasses, cracking open bones and fashioning sharp digging sticks. (Tools 2 and 4 are cores; the others are flakes.)

A 2.6-million-year-old stone flake from Gona, Ethiopia. Hominids probably used it like a knife.

But he never managed to deliver the right sort of blow. It's possible that Kanzi's arms and hands were simply not up to the anatomical challenge. On the other hand, the problem might have been in his brain, perhaps in the regions responsible for the fine control of Kanzi's hands. The problem was certainly not that Kanzi didn't understand what he was supposed to do. After failing to sharpen his rock as hominids did, Kanzi simply threw it on the floor until a flake chipped off.

Calling the stone tools of Gona "tools" may seem too generous. After all, these were not solar-powered ovens or cordless screwdrivers. But these humble stones nevertheless had a revolutionary effect on our ancestors. Hominids were no longer limited to eating fruits or insects. They could instead take advantage of the growing supply of meat from mammals grazing on the expanding grasslands. They could use their stone tools to carve flesh from carcasses or to crack open the bones to get at the calorie-rich marrow inside. And when meat was not available, hominids may have been able to find other sources of energy-rich food that had previously been off-limits, such as tubers and roots. Hominids who used stone tools still probably ate insects, but instead of delicately teasing termites out on a twig, they may have carved sharp stakes for tearing open entire nests.

This new supply of calories may have been responsible for one of the most important trends in hominid evolution: a tremendous expansion of the brain.

*Australopithecus garhi*, dating back at least 2.5 million years, may have been the first hominid to make stone tools.

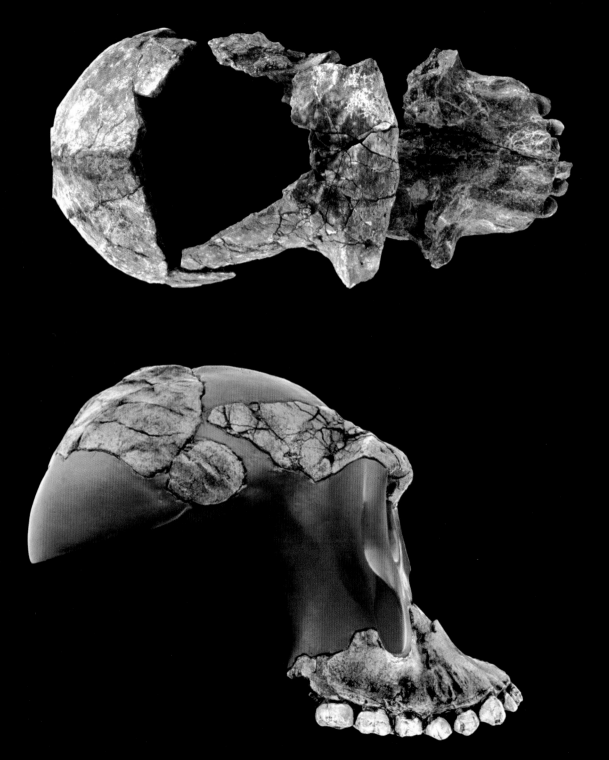

To understand what food has to do with brains, it's important to consider that brain tissue is voracious. Ounce for ounce, it consumes twelve times more oxygen than muscle. A fifth of all the calories you consume must go to your brain, even though it weighs only three pounds. It's possible that stone tools allowed hominids to find the calories to fuel a bigger brain.

The hominid brain didn't become bigger simply by inflating like a balloon, however. The change must have occurred in the genes that built hominid bodies, which scientists are just beginning to identify.

One of these genes recently came to light because when it mutates, children are born with tiny brains. This condition, known as microcephaly, shrinks the brain mainly by reducing its outer layer, the cerebral cortex. In 2002, scientists identified the defective gene that triggers microcephaly, which they dubbed ASPM. Scientists don't yet know what ASPM normally does in the developing human brain, but studies on the gene in fruit flies and mice suggest that it makes a protein that helps neurons split in two in an orderly fashion.

Evolutionary geneticists wondered if ASPM may have played an important part in the evolution of the hominid brain. For one thing, people with mutations to ASPM develop brains about as big as Lucy's. For another, these mutations have their biggest effect on the cerebral cortex, which is far larger in humans than in other apes. Perhaps, researchers speculated, ASPM evolved 2.5 to 2 million years ago, with the result that the hominid brain developed a larger cerebral cortex.

These scientists couldn't hope to study the ASPM gene of *Australopithecus afarensis*, of course, but they were still able to learn about its history. To do so, they used some newly invented methods for detecting the fingerprint of natural selection.

The crux of this method has to do with the way genes get made into proteins (see page 28). Only about 2 percent of the human genome actually contains

Reconstructed hands of *Australopithecus afarensis*.
Tool use probably influenced the evolution of hominid hands, producing fingers capable of delicate manipulation.

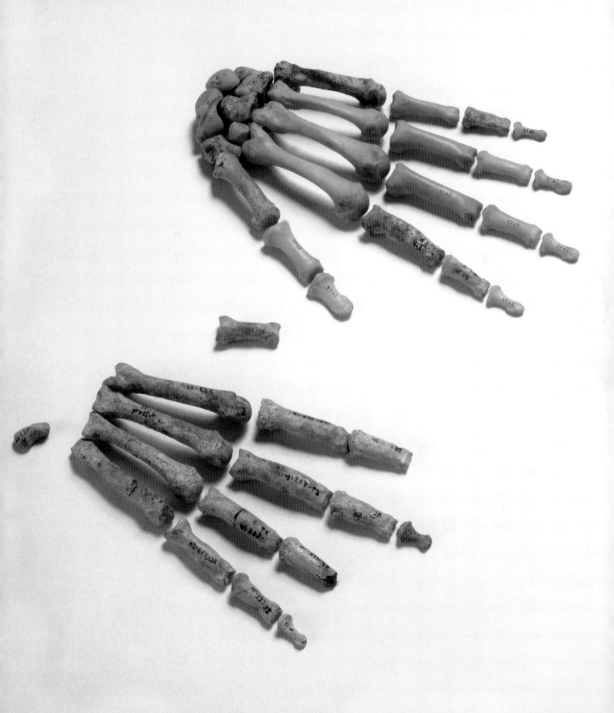

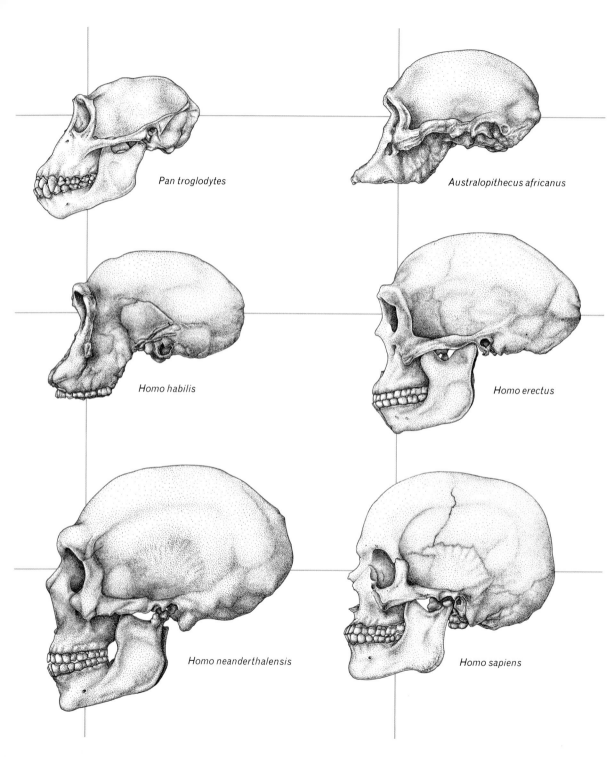

*Pan troglodytes*

*Australopithecus africanus*

*Homo habilis*

*Homo erectus*

*Homo neanderthalensis*

*Homo sapiens*

instructions for making proteins. Even within a gene sequence, there is a lot of so-called "junk DNA." While much of this material probably serves no useful function, some of it may be important to our survival in ways scientists don't yet understand.

To understand how a gene evolves, think of it as a recipe on a page of the genomic cookbook. Most of the page is filled with gibberish—AKDFJAD-KJZCXVNZCV—with the occasional moment of clarity: ADD SUGAR, SIFT FLOUR and so on. If a mutation strikes the parts of the page that contain the recipe, it can affect the final dish. Most mutations would ruin the recipe—replacing flour with water, for example. A few, however, can make the recipe better. Mutations that alter proteins so that they do a better job may be favored by natural selection and spread through a species. On the other hand, many other mutations are neither helpful nor harmful—they have no effect on the protein encoded by the gene.

Scientists can detect past episodes of natural selection by comparing the mutations that a gene carries in its coding regions and its non-coding regions. Natural selection can only favor a mutation if it alters the coding region of the gene, because only these mutations alter the structure of its protein. If a gene has many more changes to its coding region than to its non-coding region, natural selection may have been at work.

In 2004, three teams of scientists independently used this method to look at the history of the ASPM gene. They first compared versions of the gene in different primates, as well as in cats, dogs and other mammals. This let them infer ASPM's sequence in the common ancestor of these animals. Then, working forward from that ancestor, the scientists added up the number of coding and non-coding mutations that had occurred on each branch.

Early hominids had brains about as big as a chimpanzee's (*Pan troglodytes*). Humans today have brains some three times larger.

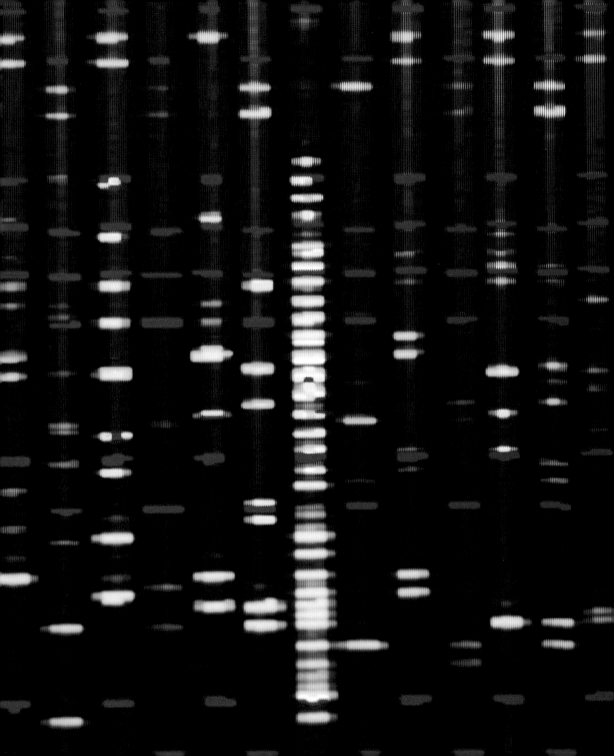

The researchers found that in non-primate mammals, ASPM has not undergone significant amounts of natural selection. But the gene began to evolve in the common ancestor of the living apes. In one of the three studies, Jianzhi Zhang of the University of Michigan found that hominids underwent an even bigger burst of ASPM evolution after they diverged from chimpanzees.

ASPM alone did not make us uniquely human. No single gene could. In 2005, some of the scientists who had discovered ASPM's evolutionary history widened their net and discovered twenty-four other genes involved in the development of the nervous system that seem to have evolved at high speed in the hominid lineage. It's likely that hundreds or thousands of other genes will also be identified as scientists take a closer look at our genome. Many of these genes may turn out to have nothing to do with the development of the brain. That's because the evolution of the human brain may have required other organs to have evolved as well.

Take the intestines. At first, they may not seem to have much to do with intelligence. But the raging appetite of our brains means that we have less energy to feed other tissue. One way to free up extra calories for the brain is to shrink other organs, and it turns out that we humans have particularly small intestines. For other primates, this is an impossible trade-off, because they need big guts to digest leaves and other tough foods. Humans, on the other hand, can survive with abbreviated intestines because we eat food far richer in energy and nutrients—thanks in large part to our tools.

This period of hominid evolution, from three million to two million years ago, will give rise to some of paleoanthropology's most exciting discoveries in coming years. It's during this time that genes, brains and tools started a complex evolutionary dance that transformed our ancestors from bipedal apes into a new species that could righly be called human.

To read the DNA sequence, scientists break up genes into fragments and place them in gel-filled columns. Switching on an electric field causes the fragments to move down the column, with heavier fragments moving more slowly. Here different fragments are shown in different colors. Scientists are using this method to discover the evolutionary history of the human brain.

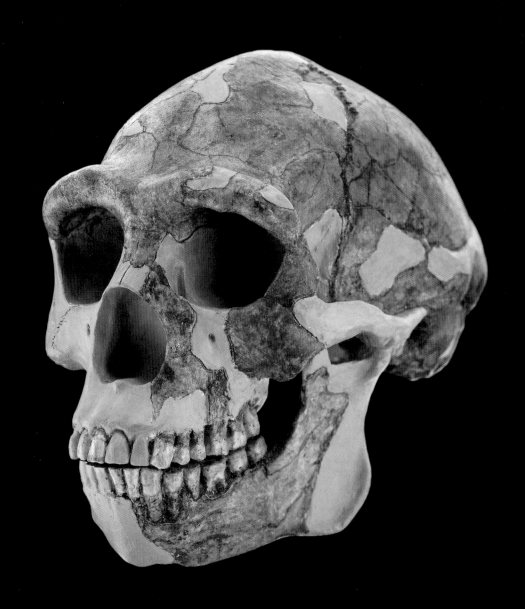

## CHAPTER FIVE

# BECOMING HUMAN

One of the occupational hazards of paleoanthropology is the occasional, intense yearning for a time-travel machine. A paleoanthropologist can glean a vast amount of information from a single fossil jaw or kneecap, but so much more remains undiscovered. Some mysteries of human evolution may be solved someday, thanks to an expedition or a brilliant new hypothesis, but some may always hang over us. If a paleoanthropologist could take just a single drive across the African landscape at a crucial moment in hominid history, we might know so much more about where we come from.

One of those crucial moments, paleoanthropologists believe, was about two million years ago. A time-traveling Land Rover moving south along the Great Rift from Ethiopia to South Africa would pass through broad grasslands and open woodlands. The scientists bouncing along inside would see vast herds of the ancient relatives of today's wildebeest and gazelles, along with the lions, leopards and other predators that ate them. They would see primates, such as the ancestors of today's baboons, walking along on the palms of their hands and climbing into trees. And, if they looked carefully, they would see hominids. The hominids might be using stone tools to crack open a leg bone from a dead wildebeest or to carve a digging stick. Some would look like small gorillas,

A 1.3-million-year-old skull of *Homo erectus* from Indonesia. It displays some of the traits that distinguish our genus *Homo* from earlier hominids, such as a large braincase, small teeth and a relatively flat face.

*Australopithecus afarensis* may have given rise to the hominid lineage that later produced our own species.

while others would be slender but still small, with long arms they may have used to climb into trees. Scientists don't quite know how many species of hominid were alive at the time; some estimates range as high as four or more. But of all the hominids our time-travelers would see, the most thrilling one—the one that would make them slam on the brakes—would have been a tall, long-legged hominid striding, or even running, across the savanna. Unlike the other hominids alive at the time, it would have been big enough to look the time travelers in the eye. The scientists would be seeing one of the earliest members of our own genus, *Homo.*

Our genus emerged at some point between three and two million years ago, but without the help of time-travel machines the details of the transformation are still murky. Some paleoanthropologists argue that Lucy's species, *Australopithecus afarensis,* gave rise to our lineage. Others look to other species, such as *Australopithecus africanus,* the South African species first discovered by Raymond Dart. In either case, the earliest fragment of a fossil that is thought to belong to *Homo* is a piece of an upper jaw dating back 2.3 million years ago, discovered in Ethiopia in 1994. Paleoanthropologists have given this scrap of bone its special place in hominid evolution, because it is shaped like later hominids' jaws and not like earlier hominids or apes.

*Homo habilis* existed from 2.3 million to 1.6 million years ago. It displayed human-like traits not seen in earlier hominids, such as the shape of its upper jaw. But it seems to have retained a number of primitive features, such as long arms and short legs.

This stone tool, dating back some time between 1.85 and 1.6 million years ago, was found in Olduvai Gorge in Tanzania, where *Homo habilis* fossils have also been found. It's possible that *H. habilis* was its creator.

Some paleoanthropologists have argued that this scrap of jaw belongs to a species called *Homo habilis*, which survived in Africa up to about 1.6 million years ago. *H. habilis* was a fascinating mix of ancient vestiges and evolutionary innovations. Its brain, which could get as big as 680 cubic centimeters, was significantly larger than Lucy's. Many stone tools have been found near *H. habilis* fossils, suggesting it was skilled at using them. But it was still relatively small, its legs short and its arms long. Some researchers who have studied its arm and hand bones even argue that it remained a skilled tree-climber.

About 1.8 million years ago, however, a new species of *Homo* that has shed many of *habilis*'s vestiges and looks much more like us appears in the fossil record. Known as *Homo ergaster*, it is estimated to have grown as tall as six feet. It had long legs, short toes and arches on its feet. Its hips were narrow and its ribs formed a small barrel, rather than the huge funnel found in chimpanzees and Lucy. Its forearms were short, and its fingers were no longer hooked. Its shoulders were low and wide. Its head had changed drastically too. Its teeth were smaller, as was its lower jaw. Its face might startle passersby on a city street, but it was much more human than

The oldest fossils of *Homo ergaster* date back 1.78 million years. It displayed many human-like traits not seen in earlier hominids, such as a larger brain and a smaller jaw.

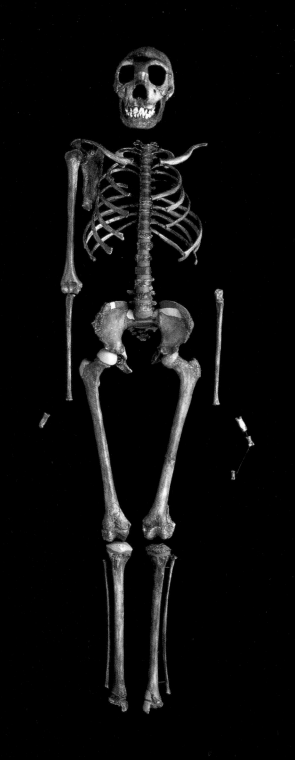

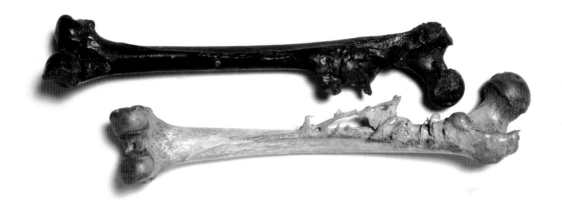

*Homo habilis*. Perhaps most important of all, *Homo ergaster*'s brain was much bigger than other hominids of the time: about two-thirds the size of a modern human's, at 870 cubic centimeters.

Many researchers are searching for a way to explain how this constellation of anatomical changes could have evolved together in our ancestors. The most recent theory, and perhaps the most intriguing, was proposed in 2004: our ancestors became runners.

Harvard University paleoanthropologist Daniel Lieberman and University of Utah biomechanics expert Dennis Bramble pointed out that we are excellent long-distance runners. Chimpanzees and other primates, by contrast, can only manage short sprints. The human body is adapted to running in ways both large

Opposite: This 1.5-million-year-old *Homo ergaster* fossil belonged to a boy. If he had reached adulthood, he would have stood over six feet tall.
Above: A diseased femur of *Homo erectus* (upper bone) is similar to a diseased femur of *Homo sapiens* (lower bone). Some scientists argue that both species are adapted for long-distance running.

and small. Long legs and stiff feet make us run faster, while a long Achilles tendon can act like a spring, storing some of the energy of each stride and releasing it in the next one. We can hold our heads steady as we run, thanks to a unique arrangement of ligaments and muscles in our necks that other primates lack. Lieberman and Bramble have studied hominid fossils for signs of these adaptations for running, and *Homo ergaster* is the earliest species to show many of them.

What were they running for? Bramble and Lieberman ask us to picture an African savanna. A lion has brought down a gazelle and has eaten its fill. A band of *Homo ergaster* sees the carcass from far away, or perhaps they spot vultures wheeling overhead. If they saunter to the carcass, hyenas or wild dogs or other hominids will beat them to it. But if they can run, they have a chance of getting there first. And any adaptations for running—for example, our tall, long-legged bodies—will be amply rewarded with extra protein and fat.

However these new hominids emerged, their new bodies posed some new challenges. As we saw in the last chapter, large brains demanded more energy. Scientists estimate that Lucy's brain used up 11 percent of the calories she took in; in *Homo ergaster*, that fraction rose to 17 percent. Stone tools would have allowed *Homo ergaster* to get more calories from marrow and meat, or perhaps even tubers. The brain's demand for energy and its sheer size also created new risks for mothers, both during pregnancy and afterward. The big heads of babies made for a tight squeeze in the birth canals of their mothers, whose hips were narrowed by natural selection for walking. Hominids' brains could only increase if babies continued to develop their brains through childhood. A chimpanzee is born with a brain 40 percent of its adult size, and by the end of its first year, that figure rises to 80 percent. A human baby, by contrast, is born with a brain only 25 percent the size of an adult's, and by its first birthday, its brain is still only 50 percent. Only at age ten does the brain reach 95 percent of its adult size.

This long period of brain development demands a lot of energy, and makes it impossible for human babies to fend for themselves. While chimpanzee babies can hold onto their mothers, human mothers have to hold their babies. Human mothers also have to provide their children with a massive supply of breast milk, and once children are weaned, they still need a steady supply of food. Juvenile chimpanzees can get some food for themselves, but the children of *Homo ergaster* may not have been able to. The staples of their diet, such as tubers or scavenged meat, could only be obtained by their parents.

Under these new conditions, natural selection may have altered the way hominids cared for their children. Earlier hominid mothers were probably entirely responsible for feeding their young, as is the case with living apes. Male chimpanzees rarely bring food to their children. Individual male and female chimpanzees do not even form long-term bonds.

A reconstruction of a Neanderthal mother caring for her child. As the hominid brain increased in size, hominid children may have needed more help from their parents.

Instead, males compete with each other for the opportunity to mate with females, while females try to mate with as many males as possible. But once hominid children became helpless, natural selection may have favored a long-term bond between parents, and fathers began bringing meat and other food to their families.

Kristen Hawkes, an anthropologist at the University of Utah, and her colleagues have pointed out that helpless children may have had an even more drastic effect on hominids: they may have given us our long lifespan. Their hypothesis is built on the fact that human females are peculiar as mammals go. Their eggs age far faster than the cells in the rest of their body. By the time a woman turns forty-five, her eggs have suffered the sort of deterioration you'd find in other organs in a woman in her eighties. This mismatch does not occur in other long-lived mammals, which can continue giving birth into their old age. A fin whale was once discovered to be pregnant in her eighties.

Hawkes and her colleagues propose that early hominids had a lifespan that was more like that of chimpanzees and other living apes. Female chimpanzees are strong and healthy until their forties, when their aging bodies start to fall apart—eggs included. Only 5 percent of adult female chimpanzees survive past the loss of their fertility. But over the course of hominid evolution, Hawkes and her colleagues argue, females began to live past menopause. Hominid females at the end of their fertility could still boost their reproductive success by helping to raise their grandchildren. They could, for example, dig up tubers so that their daughters didn't have to work as hard to find food.

Hawkes and her colleagues got the inspiration for their "grandmother hypothesis" from their studies of living groups of hunter-gatherers in Tanzania. They found that grandmothers worked hard for decades to help feed their grandchildren, pulling up nutritious roots. The researchers discovered that children without this extra help were not as healthy as those who had it. Other scientists have found that grandmothers improve the survival of children in farming societies as well. Based on these sorts of findings, Hawkes and her colleagues argue that hominid grandmothers who lived longer past menopause boosted the chances of their grandchildren surviving to adulthood. As a result, their life-extending genes spread through the hominid population.

It may be no coincidence that these tall, long-distance traveling hominids, with their big brains, stone tools and complex social lives, began to expand their range far beyond their ancestral borders. Comparing hominids to other mammals, Susan Anton of New York University has calculated that their home ranges increased by a factor of ten as they evolved into large-bodied meat-eaters. The oldest known *Homo ergaster* fossils are about 1.8 million years old; the oldest known hominid fossils outside Africa—in the former Soviet republic of Georgia and in Indonesia—are about as old. Once *Homo ergaster* appeared, its descendants seem to have spread like weeds.

Paleoanthropologists are fiercely debating what happened next. The traditional view held that the tall, human-like hominids of Africa, Asia and Europe all belonged to a single species, *Homo erectus.* Over time they evolved together into our own species, *Homo sapiens.* Now, however, very few paleoanthropologists hold this view. Many argue instead that all living humans can trace their roots to a small group of Africans who lived less than 200,000 years ago and spread out from Africa about 50,000 years ago. The lineages of hominids that were already living outside Africa became extinct, and have little or nothing to do with our own origins. (We'll get back to this part of our history in the next chapter.)

*Homo erectus* was the earliest known hominid to have spread out of Africa.

# HOMINIDS SPREAD THROUGH THE OLD WORLD

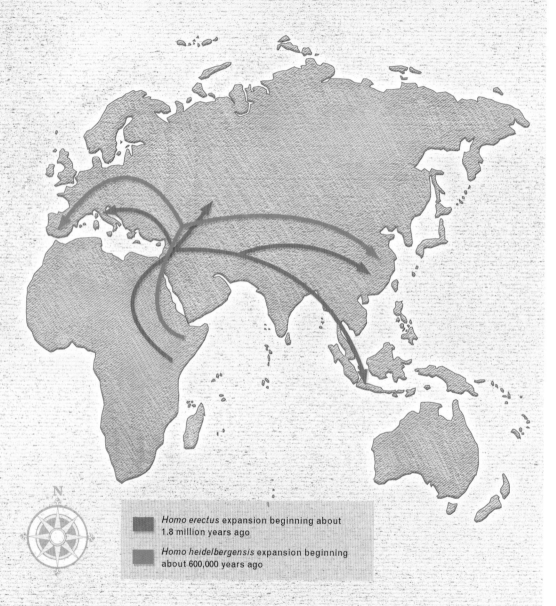

*Homo erectus* expansion beginning about
1.8 million years ago

*Homo heidelbergensis* expansion beginning
about 600,000 years ago

This new view of human evolution has led to a new debate. When the earliest hominids left Africa some 1.8 million years ago, did they branch off into one separate species, or into many separate species? The fossils don't offer a clear answer. In East Asia, paleoanthropologists have found *Homo erectus* fossils ranging from 1.8 million years ago to perhaps as recently as 30,000 years ago. Over time, the fossils suggest, East Asian hominids evolved distinctive features, such as a massive brow and ridged cranial walls. Taken on their own, those features might suggest these hominids became isolated from the hominids of Africa and evolved into a separate species. But that's hard to square with the recent discovery of a one-million-year-old hominid fossil in Africa that has more traits in common with *Homo erectus* of East Asia than with other hominids of the same age in Africa.

Different paleoanthropologists interpret this evidence differently. Jeffrey Schwartz of the University of Pittsburgh has argued that many of the fossils now called *Homo erectus* actually belong to a number of separate species. Others, such as Tim White of Berkeley, argue instead that *Homo erectus* was a single species that lived in Africa, Europe and Asia. It just happened to show a lot of variation from one place to another, which is nothing unusual for widespread animal species. Other researchers have sought an answer somewhere between these two extremes, suggesting that *Homo erectus* may have actually been a network of very isolated populations that occasionally made contact, interbred and traded genes.

The first exodus out of Africa was not the only major event in hominid evolution around this time. African *Homo erectus* also began making new tools. For the previous million years, hominids had been using the same simple stone tools found at

Beginning 1.8 million years ago, hominids expanded out of Africa in a series of waves. The fossil evidence suggests that *Homo erectus* was the earliest migrant, spreading to Europe and Asia (red arrows). Many researchers believe that a later species, *Homo heidelbergensis,* expanded out of Africa about 600,000 years ago (blue arrows). The European descendants of *H. heidelbergensis* evolved into Neanderthals. African *Homo heidelbergensis* is believed to have given rise to our own species 200,000 years ago. (The expansion of *Homo sapiens* is shown on page 129.)

Above: Acheulean hand axes were thin and symmetrical, suggesting that hominids increased their ability to plan the construction of a stone tool.
Opposite: In addition to hand axes, Acheulean technology included choppers and other kinds of tools.

Gona. But starting 1.6 million years ago, hominid tools became more sophisticated. Instead of simply chipping a rock to produce a sharp edge, hominids now sculpted rocks until they took on a predetermined shape. One type of tool, known as a hand axe, always has a teardrop-shaped form. A hominid gripping the large, rounded end of the hand axe could slice meat, whittle wood or do many other tasks. Hundreds of thousands of years later, new waves of hominid emigrants would take these tools out of Africa. They were first discovered in Europe near the town of Saint Acheul in France, and are now called Acheulean technology.

The shape of Acheulean tools suggests that African hominids had evolved a new way of thinking by 1.6 million years ago. They were now resculpting stones not simply to produce a sharp edge but also to match a shape they had in their minds. Despite this sophistication, Acheulean tools also suggest that these hominids had minds that were bafflingly different from our own. Hominids continued making this same tool kit for another 1.4 million years, and for most of that time the tools barely changed at all. Hand axes separated by a million years and a thousand miles are almost impossible to tell apart. Even if hominids evolved a new capacity for thinking about tools, they had not evolved anything remotely like human innovation.

It is not until about 600,000 years ago that the next major step in the evolution of our ancestors can be identified by paleoanthropologists. Hominid fossils from Africa that date back to around this time show clear signs of diverging from *Homo erectus*—including the size of their brain. These hominids (which some scientists call *Homo heidelbergensis*, and others call *Homo rhodesiensis*) had brains measuring about 1200 cubic centimeters, just 200 cubic centimeters shy of the size of brains in living humans.

The descendants of these big-brained hominids appear to have spread out of Africa once more, some moving as far east as China and others moving north into Europe. These early Europeans left behind some of the oldest evidence that hominids could hunt. On the island of Jersey, between France and England, the fossils of rhinos and other big mammals have been found at the bottom of cliffs, where they show signs of having been butchered. It's likely that they were killed by hominids who chased them off a precipice and then finished them off at close range. More evidence for hunting comes from the tools the hominids made. German archaeologists digging in the remains of an ancient lake discovered wooden spears dating back 400,000 years. Sharpened like javelins at both ends, the spears were between six and nine feet long. Not far away from the spear site, the archaeologists found the butchered bones of wild horses. It's possible that *Homo heidelbergensis* drove these horses into a lake and then killed them with their spears.

This type of hunting suggests that hominids had evolved the ability to cooperate in a much more sophisticated way than their ancestors. They may have been pooling a shared wisdom about the land they lived on and the animals they hunted. These hominids had also moved beyond the hand axes that their ancestors had used for

This 300,000-year-old skull found in Zambia belongs to *Homo heidelbergensis*, a species believed by some paleoanthropologists to have given rise to both Neanderthals and *Homo sapiens*. It had a significantly larger brain than *Homo erectus*.

over a million years. As far back as 300,000 years ago, *Homo heidelbergensis* was using a new technique to make stone tools. Known as Levallois tools, they were made by knocking off bits of a rock until they were left with a broad, flat shape. Then a toolmaker would deliver one sharp blow across the top of the rock, shearing off a large flake.

Despite the intricacy required to produce these new flakes, *Homo heidelbergensis* started making them in huge quantities. They used Levallois tools to cut food and plant material, and may have even attached them to the ends of spears. Despite their new tools and ability to hunt, however, other evidence suggests *Homo heidelbergensis* still did not have minds quite like our own. They show no signs of burying their dead. Paleoanthropologists have yet to find a picture they painted or a figure they carved.

While Europe could offer plenty of food for an enterprising hominid, it was also subject to devastating climate swings. The cycle of Ice Ages brought great walls of glaciers rolling as far south as England and Denmark and left much of the rest of the continent a cold desert. When the Ice Ages were at their peak, hominids survived only along the Mediterranean. During the warm intervals, they followed their game into northern Europe.

Over time natural selection altered the bodies of these European hominids in response to the harsh climate. Their legs became stubby, their chests wider, their bodies more muscled. By about 300,000 years ago, they had become markedly different from the more slender hominids in Africa. These European hominids eventually evolved into a new species by 130,000 years ago, known as *Homo neanderthalensis*, or the Neanderthals.

Of course, these European hominids were not the only species walking the Earth at this time. *Homo erectus* was thriving in East Asia, and perhaps several species were sharing Africa. This was the usual state of affairs for most of hominid history, which at this point had been unfurling for six million years.

Hartmut Thieme, a paleoanthropologist, discovered 400,000-year-old spears in Germany, including this seven-foot specimen. They are the oldest wooden weapons ever found.

But in Africa *Homo heidelbergensis* was about to give rise to a new species, which would very soon become unlike any hominid that came before. It would become the sole hominid species on the planet and would spread to continents that had never seen a hominid before. *Homo sapiens* was about to be born.

# Reconstructions

When paleoanthropologists discover a new species of ancient hominid, even a paltry collection of bone fragments can send them into ecstatic fits. Time is too cruel to expect anything more. In order to make sense of those fragments, scientists may spend years figuring out what the hominid looked like in real life.

Paleoanthropologists can rely on some general rules of biology in order to reconstruct a hominid. If they find the left half of a skull, they can safely assume that the right side was a mirror image. It's harder to extrapolate to other missing parts. A fragment from the top of a femur might be part of a long bone or a short one. In these cases, scientists turn to chimpanzees and humans as guides, because they are the hominid's closest living relatives.

But it's also important to have a rough idea of how old the hominid was when it died. A child's body proportions are dramatically different from an adult's. Paleoanthropologists can estimate the age of hominids by looking for anatomical clues. As children grow old, for example, the bones of their skull grow until they fit snugly and their milk teeth are replaced by adult teeth.

A reconstruction of a new hominid species is a scientific hypothesis. And like all scientific hypotheses, it exists to be tested. If researchers are lucky enough to find more fossils of the same species, they can compare the bones to the reconstruction to see how accurate it was. Sometimes it turns out that the original reconstruction only needs a little fine tuning. Other times it needs a drastic overhaul. In some cases, enough ambiguity remains to fuel a long-running debate.

The tools paleoanthropologists can now use to reconstruct hominids are far more sophisticated than even a decade ago. Traditionally, paleoanthropologists reconstructed hominids through sculpture. They would make casts of the original fossil bones and then meld them with elements they crafted by hand. Compare this crude work to some recent research by Christoph Zollikofer of the University of Zurich. Zollikofer and his colleagues wanted to study how the faces of Neanderthals developed as they grew up. They studied sixteen Neanderthals, estimating their ages by how developed the teeth were. Next they placed the fossils into a CT scanning device. The scientists created three-dimensional reconstructions of the bone fragments in their computer, which they could then manipulate as if they were putting together a fiendishly difficult jigsaw puzzle. When they were done, they had created a series of Neanderthal heads, including the child shown here. By comparing Neanderthals to living humans, Zollikofer and his colleagues found that from the start, the two species developed in different ways, leading to their different appearances as adults. Their research is yet another piece of evidence supporting the idea that Neanderthals did not give rise to living humans.

Putting flesh on fossil bone requires guesswork, but it can be educated guesswork. The anchors that attach muscle to bone leave telltale marks on fossils, and the size of those marks reflects the size of the muscle. Early hominids, for example, had massive muscles running from their lower jaws to their temples, while later hominids had much more modest ones. Fat deposits can be added to reconstructions by looking to humans and chimpanzees as guides.

Reconstruction experts must then choose the posture of their hominid. They can base their choice on details of the femur, hips and other bones. As for hominid skin and hair, paleoanthropologists have to make inferences. As we'll see later, early hominids were probably hairy over most of their bodies, like living apes. Hominids probably started to lose hair about two million years ago as they adapted to open grasslands. Without body hair, they also probably evolved dark skin as a protection against ultraviolet radiation.

Only by understanding what hominids looked like can paleoanthropologists get answers to some of the big questions mentioned in this book. Were early hominids bipedal? How big were hominid brains relative to their bodies? Reconstructions, it turns out, are not just eye candy for museum exhibits.

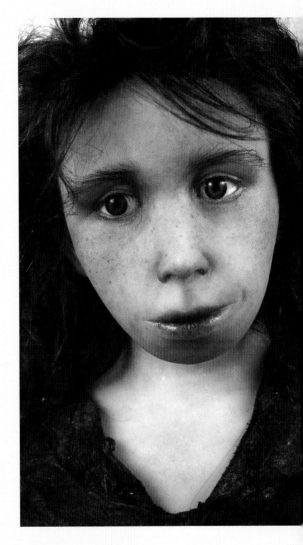

Fossils of young Neanderthals were analyzed with the help of a computer to produce a reconstruction of a Neanderthal child's face.

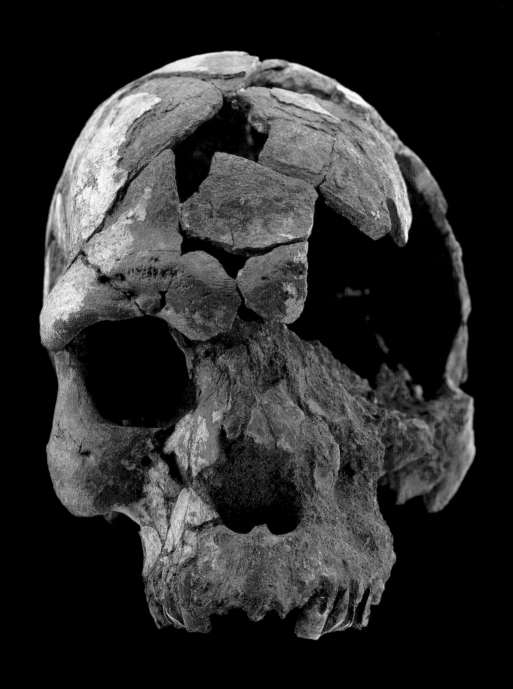

# SAPIENS

The land around the Awash River in central Ethiopia is like a museum of hominid evolution. It was here, at the dusty, barren northern end of Africa's Rift Valley that researchers discovered *Ardipithecus*, a small bipedal hominid that lived over five million years ago. Lucy's 3.2-million-year-old skeleton was found not far away. The hills of Gona nearby have yielded 2.6-million-year-old stone tools, the oldest yet found; the region has also yielded *Australopithecus garhi*, the species that may have made those tools. The tall, long-legged *Homo erectus* lived in the region a million years ago, leaving behind Acheulean hand axes. And not far away are 600,000-year-old *Homo heidelbergensis* fossils with startlingly large brains—almost as big as our own.

All this would have been quite enough to make the Awash River region one of the most remarkable places on Earth for paleoanthropology. But its fossil record does not stop there.

In 1997, Tim White of Berkeley and his colleagues were driving through a village called Herto when they noticed that recent rains had washed away the sediment around a hippo's skull. They spotted stone tools on the ground as well. Eleven days later, White and his colleagues came back to investigate. They soon discovered pieces from three hominid skulls.

In 2003 scientists reported the discovery of 160,000-year-old *Homo sapiens* fossils in the village of Herto in Ethiopia. They are among the oldest fossils of our species.

As the team assembled the pieces, they were intrigued. These were not early hominids with tiny brains and ape-like jaws. Their brains measured 1,450 cubic centimeters, as big as living humans. Older hominids had wider faces; the Herto faces were smaller, like our own. A host of other fine details in the skulls also indicated that they belonged to our own species, *Homo sapiens*. But the Herto skulls were a little unusual. They had very long faces, for example, a trait found in older hominids but missing from living humans. White and his colleagues discovered that they could put a precise date on the age of the new fossils by studying the layers of volcanic ash buried above and below them. Volcanic ash can be dated by measuring the radioactive elements it contains. The layer below the fossils is 160,000 years old, and the layer above them is 156,000 years old.

These results, published in 2003, were electrifying for two reasons. One was that before the discovery of the Herto skulls, the oldest fossils of our own species were believed to be tens of thousands of years younger. The other reason was that geneticists had been claiming since the 1980s that their studies of DNA showed that all living humans descend from a small group of Africans who lived at about that time. When the geneticists first presented this theory, hardly any hominid fossils from that period in Africa had been found. Some twenty years later, the Herto skulls fit the predictions of the geneticists like a hand in a glove.

The Herto skulls are some of the latest evidence to support the growing consensus about where and when our species evolved. But this consensus only sketches the roughest outlines of the latest stage in our evolution. The most important questions about the origin of our species remain largely unanswered.

Consider again the Herto people. Tim White's team found a number of tools alongside the fossils, including stone flakes, blades and hand axes. Some

Close examination of the *Homo sapiens* skulls found at Herto, Ethiopia, has revealed cut marks, which may have been part of funeral rituals.

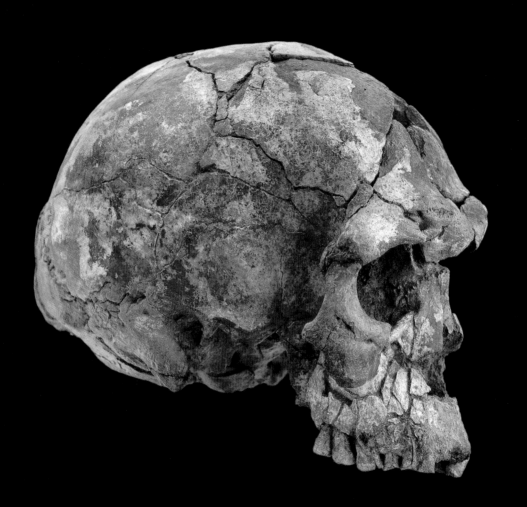

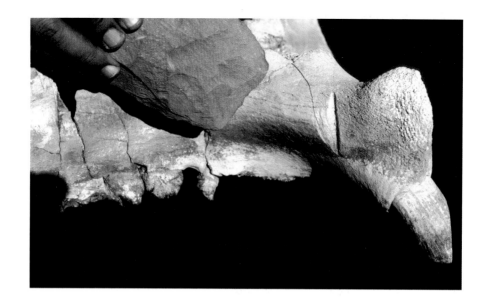

The humans of Herto used stone tools to butcher hippopotamus meat, as illustrated by this cut mark on a hippo bone discovered at the site.

of these tools had been used by hominids for hundreds of thousands of years, others for 1.4 million years. On the other hand, the researchers found no jewelry. No bone-tipped spears. No engravings of lions or elephants. In other words, the Herto people look like us anatomically, but mentally—insofar as their minds can be judged by the things they left behind—they do not seem much like us at all.

Scientists are split over how the human mind evolved past this final threshold. Some say that humans began producing art and complex tools gradually, as their culture matured. Others think that an evolutionary change to the genes that build human brains abruptly produced the extravagant creativity of modern human life.

Paleoanthropologists have long recognized that Darwin was right when he looked to Africa for our origin from apes. But until the 1990s, most concluded that our ancestors left Africa long ago. *Homo erectus* spread to Asia and Europe, where they became the Neanderthals. Despite their vast range, these hominid populations remained a single species, and gradually evolved into *Homo sapiens*.

This was a perfectly sensible interpretation of the evidence at hand as late as the 1980s—evidence that consisted mainly of fossils and tools. But in recent decades, geneticists have been able to look at a third line of evidence: the hidden record of human history encoded in our DNA.

At first this history seemed impossible to decipher. As genes pass down from one generation to the next, their origins become harder to trace. The vast majority of a person's genes reside in the nucleus of each cell. Each person carries two copies of most genes in the nucleus. But as eggs and sperm develop, they receive only one copy of each gene. It is a matter of chance which copy ends up in a given sex cell. When a sperm fertilizes an egg, their two sets of genes combine. This shuffling occurs with every generation. Any given gene you carry may have come from either of your parents, who inherited it from any one of your four grandparents, from your sixteen great-grandparents and so on. Within a couple of centuries, you have to wade through hundreds of possible donors to find the one whose gene you actually inherited.

But thirty-seven of our genes escape this generational blender. They are located not in the nucleus, but in the cell's energy-generating structures, known as mitochondria. Sperm almost never manage to deliver their mitochondria into the eggs they fertilize. So the hundreds of mitochondria in the egg become the mitochondria in every cell of the person that egg grows up to be. Your mitochondrial DNA is a nearly perfect copy of your mother's DNA, her mother's DNA and so on back through history.

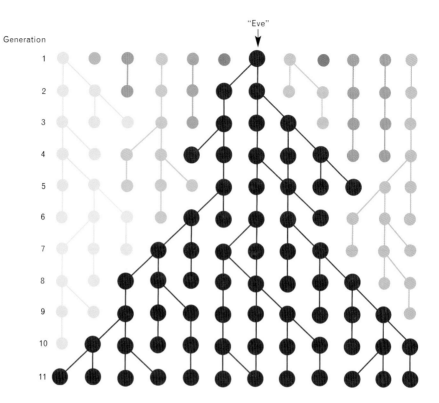

If you look back far enough in human history, all living humans can trace the ancestry of their mitochondrial DNA to a single woman (pink circle, top row). Studies on DNA from people around the world suggest this woman lived in Africa less than 200,000 years ago.

The only differences emerge when the mitochondrial DNA mutates, which it does at a slow but fairly regular rate. A mother with a mutation in her mitochondria will pass it down to her children, and her daughters will pass it down to their children in turn. In the 1980s scientists realized that they might be able to use these distinctive mutations to organize living humans into a single grand genealogy.

Scientists began to build this genealogy by comparing mitochondrial DNA from different ethnic groups. Allan Wilson of the University of California at Berkeley and his colleagues gathered DNA from 147 individuals representing Africa, Asia, Australia, Europe and New Guinea. They calculated the simplest evolutionary tree that could account for the patterns they saw. If four people shared an unusual mutation, for example, it was likely that they inherited it from a common female ancestor, rather than acquiring the mutation on their own four separate times. Wilson's team drew a tree in which almost all of the branches from all five continents joined to a common ancestor. But seven other individuals formed a second major branch. All seven of the people on this second branch were of African descent. Just as significantly, the African branches of the tree had acquired twice as many mutations as the branches from Asia and Europe. The simplest interpretation of the data was that humans originated in Africa, and that after some period of time one branch of Africans spread out to the other continents.

The subjects in Wilson's study represented ethnic groups that spanned the planet. And yet their mitochondrial DNA showed very little variation. Our entire species has less variation in our mitochondrial DNA than a few thousand chimpanzees that live in a single forest in the Ivory Coast. This low level of variation suggests that living humans all share a recent common ancestry. Wilson's team even went so far as to estimate how recent that ancestry was. Since some parts of mitochondrial DNA mutate at a relatively regular pace, they can act like a "molecular clock." Wilson and his colleagues concluded that all living humans inherited their mitochondrial DNA from a woman who lived approximately 200,000 years ago.

Scientists nicknamed this woman "mitochondrial Eve," despite the confusion that the name can create. It doesn't imply that there was only one woman alive 200,000 years ago, nor does it mean that no other contemporaries of "Eve" are ancestors of living humans. It is mainly a matter of luck that the mitochondria of "Eve's" contemporaries has disappeared from our species, while hers has survived.

Semantics aside, the discovery of mitochondrial Eve was hugely controversial. If the geneticists were right, paleoanthropologists would have to overhaul their picture of hominid evolution. Two hundred thousand years ago, Europe was already home to hominids, as was Asia. If all living humans traced their ancestry only to Africa at that time, then all the non-African hominids must have become extinct. If they had helped give rise to the living human population, mitochondrial DNA should have yielded a much older date for mitochondrial Eve.

Many paleoanthropologists greeted Wilson's work with outright hostility. But others were delighted, because they had been arguing a similar case for years. Christopher Stringer of the Natural History Museum in London, for example, had been studying the emergence of modern humans in Europe. The oldest fossils that clearly resembled living people, sometimes called Cro-Magnons, dated back 40,000 years. The Neanderthal fossils were older. Stringer had been taught that there was an unbroken line of descent from the Neanderthals to the Cro-Magnons, but his studies made him think differently. He found a much stronger link between Cro-Magnon fossils and fossils of humans in Africa dating back 100,000 years ago. Stringer proposed that Neanderthals had been an evolutionary dead end, and that Cro-Magnons were actually immigrants who had come from Africa.

The first studies by Wilson and others on mitochondrial DNA turned out to be less than bulletproof. They had not gathered enough data to eliminate the possibility that humans might have originated in Asia rather than Africa. Wilson's students continued to collect more DNA samples from a wider range of ethnic groups. Other researchers tried studying other segments of mitochondrial DNA, and today they have finished sequencing all of the DNA in the mitochondria. The results continue to point to a recent ancestor in Africa.

Other scientists have studied the DNA in the cell nucleus, in some cases with great success. Men carry a unique chromosome, called the Y, which they pass down almost unchanged to their sons. Y chromosomes are harder to study than mitochondrial DNA (in part because each cell has only one Y chromosome but thousands of mitochondria). But thanks to some smart lab work, scientists have recently been able to draw a Y-chromosome tree, and it also reveals a recent origin in Africa.

As geneticists learned how to isolate smaller and smaller amounts of DNA, they began to wonder if they could get genetic material from fossils. While most organic matter disappears from a fossil over thousands of years, they wondered if a few genetic fragments survived. In 1997, scientists discovered traces of mitochondrial DNA in a 40,000-year-old Neanderthal fossil from Germany. Since then, they've found genetic material from seven other Neanderthals across a wide geographical range, including sites in the Caucasus Mountains and Croatia.

If Neanderthals were in fact the ancestors of modern Europeans, you would expect the mitochondrial DNA of modern Europeans to be more similar to Neanderthal DNA than to other living humans. That's not what geneticists have found. In their studies, modern humans and Neanderthals form two distinct branches. The differences that have accumulated in the DNA of humans and Neanderthals suggest that they share a common ancestor who lived 500,000 years ago. And that's around the time fossils suggest that *Homo heidelbergensis* migrated from Africa to Europe.

While the original "Out of Africa" model now seems right in its broad outlines, many scientists think that it may have been too simple and stark. Some genetic studies suggest that *Homo sapiens* may have emerged from Africa in a series of waves rather than a single one. A study of one gene, published in 2004, revealed an evolutionary tree rooted in Asia, not Africa, suggesting that humans may have mated with *Homo erectus* they encountered. A 2005 study on another

Neanderthals (left) survived in Europe for several thousand years after the arrival of *Homo sapiens* (right). Studies on DNA suggest that they did not regularly interbreed.

gene hinted that humans may have interbred with Neanderthals as well. But these qualifications don't take away from the central insight of recent studies on human genes: to understand the roots of our own species, scientists must look at Africa over the last few hundred thousand years.

Unfortunately, the fossil record in Africa during this time is still murky. Paleo-anthropologists know that hominids were living across much of Africa: from the Mediterranean shores of Morocco to the Cape of Good Hope in South Africa. Yet researchers have only managed to give serious scrutiny to a handful of these sites. It is even hard to figure out how old these sites are. Few contain volcanic-ash beds, which can be dated easily. Carbon 14, which is found in trace amounts in organic matter, also records the passage of time, but only up to about 40,000 years ago.

Without these clocks at their disposal, paleoanthropologists have to turn to other methods. One technique, known as optically stimulated luminescence, allows scientists to measure how long it has been since a buried piece of soil or sand has seen the light of day. Although luminescence and other new methods show a lot of promise, they still have plenty of kinks to be worked out. As a result, paleoanthropologists often wind up with estimates that span over 30,000 years. That's not a bad margin of error for scientists who are studying the apes that lived ten million years ago. But when they are studying fossils and tools from the past 300,000 years, these margins sow confusion.

Despite these uncertainties, paleoanthropologists are beginning to get a clearer picture of hominid evolution in Africa over the past half-million years. The big-brained hominids that branched off from *Homo erectus* gradually acquired more of the features found in our own species. African skulls dating back 260,000 years show that their faces were becoming flatter than their ances-tors, and their foreheads were becoming higher. On the other hand, these African hominids still had the thick braincase walls and broad cheeks of their predeces-sors. Some of these skulls may have belonged to short-lived species that became extinct. Other hominids evolved into *Homo sapiens*. The Herto fossils suggest that our own species was firmly established in Africa by 160,000 years ago. In

2005, another team of researchers pushed the fossil record of our species even farther back when they redated *Homo sapiens* fossils discovered in Ethiopia in the 1960s. Originally dated to 130,000 years ago, they are now believed to be 195,000 years old.

The tools made by Africans during this time were changing as well. By 280,000 years ago, they had begun fashioning long stone blades. Later they learned how to make finely crafted points. These Africans also left behind ocher, a red pigment that many living African peoples use for artwork and to decorate their own bodies. (Some researchers think this ancient ocher was used to tan hides. That wouldn't indicate the sort of abstract thought required for artwork, but it's still a sophisticated behavior.)

Hominids had been making tools for well over two million years at this point, but they had shown almost no creativity or individuality in their handiwork. Now human creativity was beginning to accelerate at an unprecedented pace. The Herto people, to give just one example out of many, made blades out of obsidian. They also made the more traditional rounded stone flakes. The bones of butchered hippos and other big mammals tell us that the Herto people were using their tools to remove meat from animals that they probably hunted. But they also used their tools on their own dead.

Tim White and his colleagues found only the skulls of humans at Herto, yet they found much more complete skeletons of other animals. That discrepancy hints that someone removed the heads of the Herto people shortly after they died and brought them to the spot where they were found. Close inspection of the skulls revealed cut marks at their bases. It seems that the lower jaws were intentionally removed, along with some of the bone around the foramen magnum, the

Discovered in 1967 near the Omo River in Ethiopia, this skull and other *Homo sapiens* fossils were initially estimated to be 130,000 years old. But in 2005, more sophisticated dating techniques revealed that the Omo fossils are actually 195,000 years old, making them the oldest fossils known of our species.

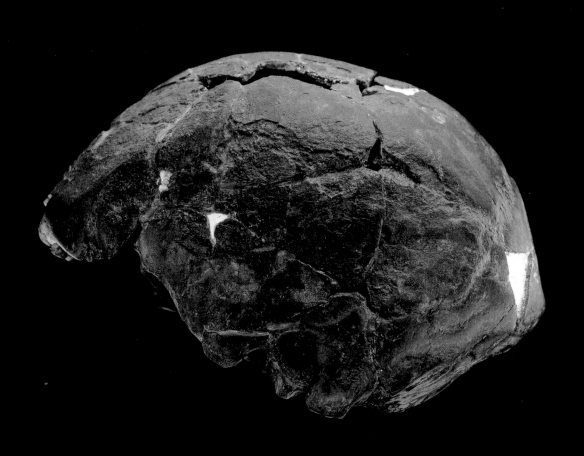

In South Africa, scientists have found evidence of symbolic thought dating back 77,000 years. A human ground this slab of ocher to produce a flat surface and then etched a crisscross pattern on it with a stone tool.

hole through which the spinal cord leaves the head. The jagged edges of the hole were then polished smooth. The skulls of Herto suggest that the earliest humans performed rituals for their dead. Just what those rituals were, or represented, scientists may never discover.

The Herto people lived during some of the harshest conditions in the past

300,000 years. The Earth's climate was undergoing massive swings, and Africa lurched between periods of wet and dry weather. Clues from our genes suggest that this change was especially hard on our ancestors. By measuring variations in the DNA of living humans, scientists can estimate how many ancestors gave rise to them. Around the time that the Herto people lived, the population of our entire species may have dwindled down to a few thousand individuals. Scientists call such population crashes "bottlenecks." During bottlenecks, evolution can speed up, because it takes less time for new genes to spread through a small population. These new genes may produce new adaptations or may turn a population into an entirely new species. It's possible that our own species was born out of such a harrowing transformation.

Humans gradually rebounded from this bottleneck. They settled in new regions of Africa and took up new livelihoods. By 125,000 years ago, some humans had settled along the coast and were fishing, collecting oysters and even hunting seals. As African humans spread, they left behind evidence that they were beginning to take on the trappings of modern human culture. They appear to have traded tools along long-range networks that could span hundreds of miles. Paleoanthropologists measure this trade by calculating the distances between where they find tools and the nearest places where those tools could have been made. In Tanzania, for example, they have found obsidian blades in a cave dating back 100,000 to 130,000 years. The closest deposits of obsidian are 200 miles away. Today, a single band of foraging people may transport tools fifty miles in their search for food. But the ancient Tanzanian obsidian blades moved four times farther. To travel such long distances, they must have been traded from one band of humans to another.

During this time, African technology began to take on regional styles. A million-year-old hand axe from South Africa is pretty much identical to a million-year-old hand axe in Ethiopia. But 70,000 years ago, *Homo sapiens* in Africa were making different sorts of tools in different parts of the continent. In the Congo Basin, for example, humans made their stone points long and thin, while in parts of South Africa, they made them small and squat. In these styles, some paleoanthropologists see signs that modern humans were sharing information with one another, passing on wisdom to friends and children. That wisdom varied with the ecological conditions in Africa, which led to regional styles.

New evidence even suggests that Africans at this time were also branching out from practical tools to art and jewelry. In South Africa, paleoanthropologists have found 77,000-year-old pieces of red ocher that have been engraved with crisscrossing lines. In the same cave, they have also found 75,000-year-old sea shells that appear to have been bored to wear on a necklace.

All of these tokens indicate that after six million years and some twenty species, hominid evolution had now produced a truly remarkable animal. But tens of thousands of years would pass before they gained a title that is truly rare: the single hominid left on Earth.

The same site in South Africa that yielded the crisscross ocher shown on page 114 has also produced what appear to be the oldest known ornaments—thirty-nine snail shells with holes drilled through them, perhaps for a necklace. They are 75,000 years old.

# Language

We live in a sea of words, immersing ourselves in cable news, talk radio, cell phone conversations, electronic mail, whispers, screams and an endless supply of instruction manuals. Yet as important as language is to our existence, it is one of the most puzzling features of human evolution. It is at once complex and ephemeral. You can express an infinite number of ideas with language, and yet those ideas drift away in the breeze as soon as you utter them. The record of writing reaches back 5,500 years, but the spoken word has no hope of fossilizing. In 1866, the *Société de Linguistique* in France decided that the subject could only inspire futile speculation and officially banned any discussion of the origin of language.

For over a century, scientists generally heeded the *Société*'s advice. That has changed in recent decades. Now the evolution of language is one of the most exciting fields, attracting not just linguists but also neuroscientists, primatologists, geneticists and even mathematicians.

One line of evidence for the evolution of language is language itself. Steven Pinker of Harvard University has forcefully argued that the structure of language demonstrates that it is a complex adaptation produced by natural selection, just like the eye or the foot. Language is not just a cultural tradition that emerges from our all-around intelligent brains, like the ability to play chess or plant corn. Instead, the human brain contains networks of neurons that specialize in language. Some types of brain damage can selectively wipe out a person's ability to speak or understand grammar, leaving their powers of reasoning otherwise untouched. Just as all people have eyes and feet, all people use language. And just as everyone's eyes and feet developed in the same way, language develops in children along pretty much the same set of milestones. Even when children aren't properly taught a language, their language faculty is so powerful that they can invent one for themselves. In the 1980s, for example, deaf Nicaraguan children who were taught a crude set of signs for letters spontaneously invented a language of their own, complete with grammar and syntax.

Pinker believes that natural selection originally produced language as an adaptation that helped humans thrive in the "cognitive niche." Only humans use cause-and-effect reasoning to overcome the defenses of plants and animals (poisons, thorns, teeth) to get food and other resources. Language allows humans to translate this reasoning into signals that they can exchange with one another. Humans can use language to teach their children how to fish, or to provide information to a stranger in exchange for a new spear. Any gene that enhanced this information exchange—producing syntax, for example, which allowed the order of words to convey meaning—boosted the reproductive success.

Other scientists see language differently. Marc Hauser, also of Harvard, and his colleagues have argued that most of the components of language may have already been in place in our ancestors millions of years before the first hominid made a noise. They point out that living primates and other animals have many of these abilities, which makes it likely that our common ancestors had those skills as well. The human brain, for example, contains neurons that are finely tuned to human speech. They respond strongly to the sound of people speaking but barely register other sounds. Scientists were so impressed by this discovery in the 1950s that they declared it to be a unique human adaptation linked to language. But later scientists discovered that monkeys are tuned to their own voices, as are birds and even chinchillas. It is useful for other animals to quickly recognize the sound of their own species, even if they are only communicating simple grunts or chirps. Hauser and his colleagues see the same overlap in other ingredients of human language—such as conceptual representation and the ability to produce sounds that refer to things or other members of one's own species.

What human language has that cannot be found in other animals, Hauser argues, is a hierarchy, in which one phrase can branch off from another thanks to the syntax of a sentence. But this capacity (known as recursion) is not special to stringing together words. Recursion is just as helpful to solving many complex problems made up of interrelated parts. It's possible that recursion evolved as an adaptation for some other

aspect of human life, such as navigating long distance. Fortuitously, it might then have helped organize human communication into something far more complex. Far from a fine-tuned product of natural selection, language might be a useful byproduct of other adaptations.

Just when all this happened, neither Hauser nor Pinker is eager to speculate. It's a safe bet that the common ancestor of chimpanzees and humans was no more gifted than today's chimpanzees, judging from brain size alone. By 50,000 years ago, humans almost certainly had full-blown language. As we'll see in the next chapter, humans at that time started leaving behind cave paintings, signs of trade networks spanning hundreds of miles and intricately designed tools that couldn't have been mastered by pure imitation. That leaves over six million years in which language may have arisen. It may have gradually emerged, or burst forth only recently in our history. If it occurred in the last 200,000 years, that would mean Neanderthals couldn't understand complex language, for example—which might prove to be one factor that drove them to extinction.

Paleoanthropologists have struggled to pin some dates to the rise of language. Many have tried to find some anatomical feature that can survive in a fossil bone that is a clear sign that its owner could talk. But these hallmarks have proven surprisingly hard to discover. For a while, researchers thought they found a good one in a small hole in the skull. The hole allows a nerve to pass out of the brain to the tongue, and in humans it is large. The hole might have increased during

Nicaraguan children use a sign language they invented. Their ability to invent a new language shows how deeply ingrained language is in our brains.

hominid evolution as our ances-tors became more nimble with speech. But more detailed studies have revealed a wide range of hole sizes in both humans and apes, with no clear division between the different species.

If fossils fail to help, our DNA may offer some clues. In 2001, a team of geneti-cists at Oxford University discovered the first gene with a clear role in language. They were studying a Pakistani family in which many mem-bers had trouble talking because they couldn't control their mouth muscles and they also had difficulty understanding grammar. This language impairment ran in the family as a hereditary trait, like blue eyes or the ability to curl your tongue. Searching through the genomes of the family members, the geneticists discovered that those who had trouble talking all carried mutated ver-sions of the same gene, which the scientists named FOXP2.

The geneticists teamed up with Svante Pääbo at the University of Munich, who is an expert at detecting signs of past natural selection in genes. Many mammals, they noted, have related versions of FOXP2, though no one knows what it does for

them. But the investigators found that after the human lineage split from that of the chimpanzee, FOXP2 underwent rapid evolution. In fact, minor variations in the present-day forms of the gene point to its spread throughout our species less than 200,000 years ago.

Of course, the mutation of a single gene could not have produced human language all at once. Geneticists are looking at other families with different language impairments in the hopes of finding other genes that are essential for lan-guage. It's possible that these genes played an important role in the rise of the modern mind 50,000 years ago, as suggested by Richard Klein of Stanford University. Or perhaps they built language up slowly over hundreds of thousands, or even millions, of years. Whichever turns out to be the case, no one will be banning papers on the results.

# THE LAST WAVE

The first venture our species took out of Africa apparently ended in failure. Fossil discoveries suggest that about 130,000 years ago anatomically modern humans migrated through the Sinai Peninsula to the eastern coast of the Mediterranean, a region known as the Levant. (Today this region includes parts of Turkey, Lebanon, Syria, Jordan, Israel and Egypt.) The humans who made this migration looked like us and had brains as big as our own. They used those brains to make sophisticated thin stone flakes for hunting, scavenging or gathering plants. These people also transported shells from the coast to over twenty miles inland, perhaps to use as ornaments. They showed a profound appreciation for life and death, which they demonstrated by carefully burying their dead in caves, sometimes placing a boar jaw or the antler of a red deer on the bodies. We can almost imagine what it would be like to be these people, because they seem so close to ourselves.

These African migrants settled in the Levant for thousands of generations. But then they vanished from the fossil record. No one knows exactly what happened to them, but what is clear is that once again *Homo sapiens* became a species restricted to Africa. The Levant, however, did not become devoid of humans. Another species of humans—the Neanderthals—swept down into the

*Homo sapiens* acquired an unprecedented ability to think symbolically, as seen in these 22,000-year-old images from the Cussac Cave in France.

Levant from Europe, and would thrive in the region for 30,000 years, until *Homo sapiens* finally returned.

The temptation is always strong to see our own species as the pinnacle of evolution. But such an arrogant view of life makes it hard to understand how a population of *Homo sapiens* could be replaced by a supposedly inferior group of cave men. In fact, Neanderthals were in many ways our equals, and in some ways our betters. Only by recognizing the success of Neanderthals can we begin to understand why we are the only surviving hominid species left on Earth and they are not.

About 500,000 years ago, the ancestors of Neanderthals expanded into Europe, a continent that was regularly ravaged by Ice Age glaciers. At the peak of each Ice Age, the northern reaches of Europe were covered by ice and much of the lower latitudes of Europe were reduced to cold deserts and grasslands. But even under the harshest conditions, Europe remained home to big mammals, such as mammoths, wooly rhinoceros and Irish elk. If hominids could withstand the cold, they could find plenty to eat.

Earlier Ice Ages apparently were too harsh for hominids to survive in Europe, but the ancestors of the Neanderthals met the challenge. They likely evolved from *Homo heidelbergensis*, developing a distinctive body. Their skulls were long and low, with large brow ridges. But unlike the brow ridges in most other hominids, those of Neanderthals were full of air spaces, and therefore much lighter. Their faces were long, their noses huge. They were stocky and muscular; paleoanthropologists estimate that a Neanderthal weighed 30 percent more than a living human of the same height. Picture an Olympic shot-putter with Cyrano de Bergerac's nose.

The cold climate of Europe probably helped shape much of this anatomy. The huge nasal cavities of Neanderthals may have warmed and moistened the cold,

This skull, dating back 90,000 to 100,000 years ago, belonged to a *Homo sapiens* woman who lived in Israel. She may have belonged to the first expansion of modern humans out of Africa. This expansion ended about 80,000 years ago, and modern humans didn't return to the eastern Mediterranean until about 50,000 years ago.

Neanderthals had brains as large as those of living humans. Yet paleoanthropologists suspect that their minds didn't work quite the same way as ours.

dry air they inhaled. Their stocky bodies released less heat than if they had slender limbs. You can see this same principle at work in the bodies of living humans. People who have lived for thousands of years in colder climates, such as Eskimos and Lapps, have shorter shins relative to their thighs, while people who live in hot climates have much longer ones. (This even applies to pygmies—they may not be tall, but they have slender limbs to help cope with tropical heat.)

Neanderthal bodies were also adapted for another function: to hunt. Their arms and hands were specialized for gripping, delivering powerful thrusts and withstanding strong shocks—just the adaptations that could help hunters who kill big game with handheld spears. Neanderthals also withstood a wide range of insults, from stab wounds to broken bones to arthritis. Facing these sorts of traumas, Neanderthals rarely lived past forty-five years.

But an Ice Age hunter needed more than brawn to survive. Neanderthals had brains as big as living humans, and the evidence they left behind suggests they were very intelligent, at least in their own way. They were experts in animal behavior, often hunting particular animals such as red deer or bison. Neanderthals must have been able to work together to hunt, whether they were ambushing a rhino or

Reconstruction of a Neanderthal skeleton (left), compared with *Homo sapiens* (right). Neanderthals were stockier than *Homo sapiens*. Their rugged anatomy may have been an adaption to hunting big game in the cold climate of Ice Age Europe.

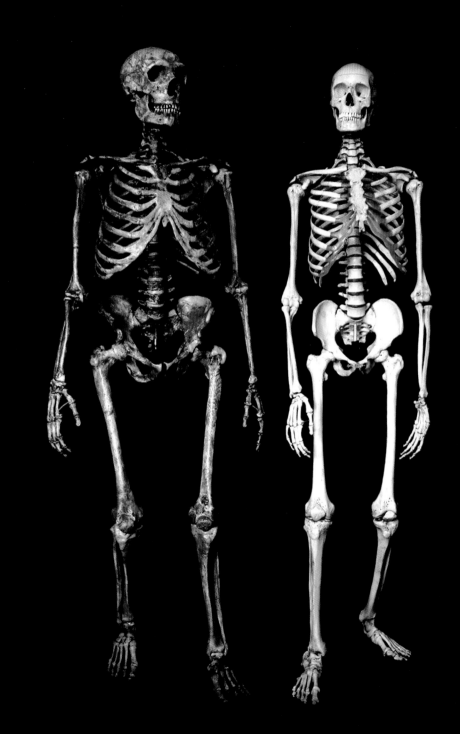

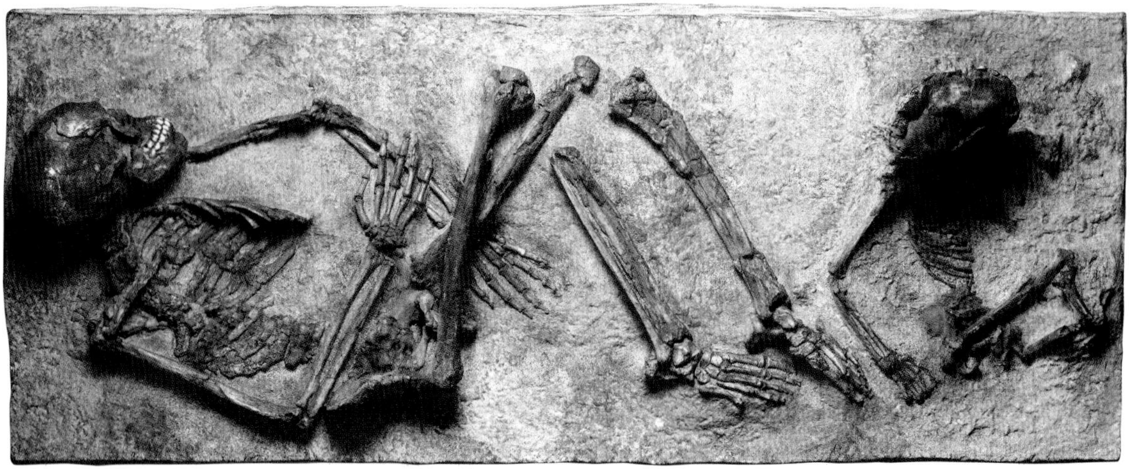

These 90,000- to 100,000-year-old fossils are of a *Homo sapiens* mother and child, in what appears to be a ritual burial in a cave in Israel. The elaborate care for the dead shown here is not found in other hominids.

driving a herd of horses off a cliff. And Neanderthals needed to make tools to kill and butcher these animals. They were experts at making Levallois stone flakes in different shapes for different purposes. For instance, they could use the blades to carve spears, which they then hardened in fires. At the end of the spears they added other stone blades.

It's harder to figure out the social life of Neanderthals, but scientists have found a few clues. Neanderthals buried their dead, although there's not much evidence that they placed antlers or other objects that carried some symbolic value on the bodies. There's almost no evidence that they identified themselves as part of groups by wearing jewelry. They lived in small groups, finding shelter in caves rather than in huts of their own making. And their tools didn't wind up very far from where they were made, which suggests that Neanderthal groups didn't trade with one another. Instead, they kept mostly to themselves.

Neanderthals and humans had a lot in common between 150,000 and 50,000 years ago. Both species were adapted to a particular environment and didn't stray from it. The ancestors of living humans were restricted to Africa, and they were tall and thin, perhaps in order not to build up too much heat in the tropical sun. They made their first known foray out of Africa into the Levant 130,000 years ago, when a warmer, wetter climate was making the Levant ecologically more like Africa. Many African plants and animals spread north through the Sinai Peninsula, and humans followed suit. When the climate became cooler and drier about 80,000 years ago, some scientists have argued that humans retreated back into Africa proper.

Neanderthals shifted in a similar way. When the glaciers retreated, they moved north through Europe. When a new Ice Age began, they moved south, and some time after 80,000 years ago they spread all the way down to the Levant. They settled into this new home and remained there for thousands of years, where game was plentiful and the climate hospitable.

But this pattern was shattered 50,000 years ago. *Homo sapiens* returned to the Levant, despite the fact that the Ice Age was advancing, not retreating. Neanderthals retreated into Europe, and modern humans moved in after them. Somehow our species had ceased being subject to the vagaries of climate. They found a secret that would ultimately let them sweep across the entire planet.

Neanderthals made stone tools by fracturing a rock into many small flakes. They may have used the tools for butchering meat, cutting plant material or as spear points.

Studies on human DNA are allowing scientists to begin mapping the spread of our species. Before about 50,000 years ago, when humans successfully migrated out of Africa, they were already beginning to diverge into distinct populations. Along the way, these populations took on distinctive mutations. Consequently, there's far more genetic variation among living Africans than among the rest of the human population.

The migrations out of Africa consisted of relatively few people. One piece of evidence for this exodus is the fact that all men from outside Africa carry the same mutation on the Y chromosome known as M168. The best explanation for this pattern is that M168 arose in Africans whose descendants colonized the other continents. Variations in the DNA that surrounds the M168 marker suggest that it first arose between 56,000 and 81,000 years ago.

Studies of DNA also suggest that the M168 people spread out from Africa in at least two waves. The earlier wave traveled from Eastern Africa into the Arabian Peninsula. From there, humans continued eastward, following the coast of South Asia. Some of the best evidence for this southern migration comes from isolated people whose genes have not been blurred much by intermarrying with outsiders. On the Andaman Islands in the Bay of Bengal, hunter-gatherers have resisted assimilating with mainland populations for centuries. Studies on their DNA show that their roots reach far back in time, close to the origin of all living humans. This southern wave did not stop with the Andaman Islands, however, but kept rolling along. It reached southeast Asia, where one branch of people migrated to Australia and New Guinea, while other branches moved along the eastern coast of Asia.

Based on evidence from fossils and DNA, the current scientific consensus is that our species evolved in Africa 200,000 years ago. *Homo sapiens* initially expanded through Africa (pink). An expansion into the Levant (yellow) ended about 80,000 years ago. Later, Africans spread into southern Asia (orange). The same group appears to have also spread into central Asia, Siberia and Europe (green). Several different groups appear to have moved from Asia into the New World roughly 20,000 years ago.

# MIGRATION OF HOMO SAPIENS

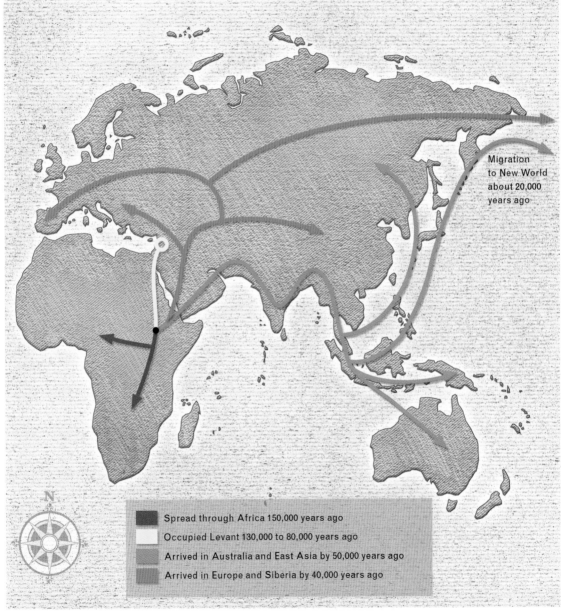

Migration
to New World
about 20,000
years ago

Spread through Africa 150,000 years ago

Occupied Levant 130,000 to 80,000 years ago

Arrived in Australia and East Asia by 50,000 years ago

Arrived in Europe and Siberia by 40,000 years ago

Thousands of years later, the DNA studies suggest, a branch of this migration moved north, into the Levant and Central Asia. Over time this branch spread west into Europe and east into Siberia.

Scientists are still working to pin down the precise timing of these migrations. The oldest fossils of modern humans outside Africa are all younger than 50,000 years old. In the Near East, fossils of *Homo sapiens* date back 47,000 years. In Australia, the oldest are about 40,000 years, although human tools date back to 50,000 years. In Europe, fossils of *Homo sapiens* turn up about 40,000 years ago. Of course, this evidence can't pinpoint the exact time when humans spread to various parts of the world, because a fossil only reveals the *latest* possible date at which humans may have arrived at a particular place. The timing of the southern wave of human migration may be particularly hard to pin down, because it appears to have moved along the coast. After the end of the last Ice Age, 12,000 years ago, the melting glaciers drowned large stretches of coastline. If there are fossils of older migrants waiting to be discovered, paleoanthropologists may need scuba gear to find them.

The fossils of these migrants offer few clues as to what sparked their spread. Their brains were no bigger than those of the Herto humans who lived over 100,000 years earlier. But these people were clearly different. Consider what it took to get to Australia. Australia is separated from southeast Asia by a great expanse of water. During the Ice Age, the distance was smaller because so much water was locked up in glaciers. But 50,000 years ago humans would have still faced a voyage across over fifty miles of open ocean to get to Australia. They must have built sea crafts rugged enough for the trip, an endeavor that went far beyond fashioning a spear or lighting a fire.

To make boats and other inventions, humans needed tools. Africans had been making increasingly sophisticated tools for over 100,000 years, but many

A 25,000-year-old sculpture of a bear from the Czech Republic.

paleoanthropologists believe that humans crossed a creative threshold 50,000 years ago. It was around then, for example, that humans began making small blades out of quartz that may have been the first arrowheads. They fashioned fish hooks and left behind the earliest traces of manmade shelters.

Earlier Africans had produced ornaments and artwork, but after 50,000 years ago, human self-expression shifted into high gear. People carved beads and pendants out of horn, ostrich eggs and snail shells. They carved figurines of bears and deer from bone. Their artistic expression flowered into huge paintings, whether deep inside the caves of southern France or on above-ground rocks in Australia.

Paleoanthropologists are exploring a number of hypotheses for this unprecedented combination of new technology, self-expression and population boom. They generally agree that ultimately some sort of biological change in our ancestors made it possible, but they disagree about when it occurred. You can roughly split their hypotheses into two categories—the "long-fuse" hypotheses and the "short-fuse" hypotheses.

Alison Brooks of George Washington University and Sally McBrearty of the University of Connecticut have made the strongest arguments for the long fuse. They believe that the transformation of human culture began as long ago as 300,000 years, in the African lineage of hominids that produced *Homo sapiens*. They point out that by 280,000 years ago African hominids were already making blades and using ocher pigments. Other hallmarks of modern behavior then began to emerge in Africa at an accelerating pace.

This acceleration of invention, McBrearty and Brooks argue, is the result of cultural change. The fact that people only began covering cave walls with huge paintings and building sophisticated spear-throwers out of antler bone 40,000 years ago didn't mean that these people carried new brain-boosting genes that didn't exist in people 200,000 years earlier. To McBrearty and Brooks, that would be as absurd as saying that Isaac Newton was biologically incapable of driving a car because he lived three centuries before it was invented.

McBrearty and Brooks argue that the social and cultural conditions of early humans drove the rise of modern human behavior. When early *Homo sapiens* in Africa began to make new tools, they were able to get more food, which increased their chances of surviving and having children. Their population began to rise and they were able to spread to new habitats, such as tropical forests and coasts. But the climate then gradually slid into an Ice Age, making the supply of food less abundant in Africa and elsewhere. Africans were forced

A 24,000-year-old sculpture of a woman's head found in France.

A 26,000-year-old bone needle found in France. By inventing new tools such as needles, humans may have withstood the Ice Ages of Europe, outcompeting the Neanderthals.

to invent new tools to survive and to form more complex social networks. Small groups of humans joined together in alliances, exchanging precious tools and food. A modern analogy to this practice may be found among the San people of southern Africa. Hunting and foraging in the Kalahari Desert, they live at the edge of survival. Individual San give gifts to other people from other groups; they know that later they can expect a gift back.

Where McBrearty and Brooks (and many others) see gradual change, others see a revolution. Paleoanthropologist Richard Klein of Stanford University has made the strongest case for the "short-fuse" hypothesis. In his view, the evidence of modern minds from before 50,000 years ago is either questionable or inconsequential. Klein thinks that a new burst of behavior swept through our species at that time, and that was the result of changes to human DNA. Some kind of biological change occurred to the brains of certain Africans that allowed them to think in a new way. In 2002, scientists identified a gene that might fit Klein's hypothesis. Known as FOXP2, it is crucial for human language. It appears to have undergone intense natural selection sometime in the past 200,000 years (see page 119).

*Homo sapiens* developed an unprecedented creativity, as displayed in the tools they made. Humans began using a wide range of materials, such as the quartz shown here, and created new kinds of tools, including arrowheads.

This debate about how modern human behavior emerged is intimately tied up with another, darker mystery: what happened to the other hominids?

The Neanderthals seem to have retreated as *Homo sapiens* advanced out of Africa. They disappeared from the Levant when modern humans arrived there about 50,000 years ago. As *Homo sapiens* gradually moved north and west, they began to settle in the Neanderthal's core territory: Europe. Modern humans arrived in Europe at least 40,000 years ago, but Neanderthals appear to have survived for over 10,000 years in their company. Paleoanthropologists don't know if the newly arived *Homo sapiens* fought with Neanderthals or made peaceful contact. One fascinating clue comes from a French cave called Grotte du Renne, near the town of Arcy-sur-Cure. There explorers discovered thirty-six necklace ornaments made from the bones of swans and other animals. Further research revealed that the ornaments, dating back some 33,000 years, were made while Neanderthals lived in the cave. Stranger still, the tools that the Neanderthals appear to have used were made in a distinctive style (called Chatelperronian) that characterizes the tools of modern humans who lived in France at the time. Neanderthals apparently imitated their *Homo sapiens* neighbors, suggesting that they had at least some ability to think symbolically and copy the work of others.

On the whole, Neanderthals seem to have not been able to compete with their new neighbors. Modern humans may have lived in larger groups than Neanderthals, and may have been able to take over more and more of the best sites for finding food and shelter. In their search for game, they weren't limited to sneaking up on animals and spearing them; they could use other weapons, such as spear throwers. And thanks to their long-range networks of trade and communication, modern humans could withstand the rapid climate changes that Europe underwent at the time. Modern humans appear to have moved farther into

Over the past 300,000 years, *Homo sapiens* and their ancestors have shown a growing sophistication and complexity in the tools, art and ornaments they've produced. Scientists are divided over what drove this change.

# MILESTONES IN THE RISE OF MODERN HUMANS

**Thousands of Years Ago (kya)**

**300,000**

**280 kya** Stone blades and ocher pigments used by ancestors of *Homo sapiens* in Africa

**250,000**

**200,000**

**195 kya** Oldest fossils of *Homo sapiens* found in Ethiopia

**150,000**

**140 kya** Evidence of long-distance exchange and shell fishing in Africa

**130 kya** *Homo sapiens* moves into the Levant

**100,000**

**80 kya** *Homo sapiens* occupation of the Levant ends, replaced by Neanderthals
**77 kya** Ornamental shells and geometrical engravings made in South Africa

**About 50 kya** *Homo sapiens* expands out of Africa

**50,000**

**41 kya** Oldest evidence of humans in Europe

**40,000**

**36 kya** Oldest European cave art

**33 kya** Neanderthal-made ornaments suggest Neanderthals imitated *Homo sapiens*

**30,000**

**28 kya** Neanderthals become extinct
**27–53 kya** Estimated age of the youngest *Homo erectus* fossils in Indonesia

**20,000**

**About 20 kya** *Homo sapiens* moves from Asia into North America

**18 kya** Youngest known fossils of *Homo floresiensis*

**10,000**

Europe, while Neanderthals retreated to the Pyrenees and other remote mountainous areas, where they finally disappeared.

The fate of *Homo erectus* is much more mysterious. Ironically, it is puzzling in part because scientists discovered *Homo erectus* so long ago. Today, when paleoanthropologists dig up a fossil, they make very careful notes about the rocks in which the fossils are embedded. They look for evidence that the fossils and the rocks are of the same age; sometimes fossils are dislodged from their original resting places and become embedded in much younger rocks. The scientists also take care to note whether the fossils are buried close to layers of volcanic ash, which can be precisely dated. This sort of care was not common in the late 1800s and early 1900s, when paleoanthropologists found the first *Homo erectus* fossils in Indonesia. Instead, they simply dug up the bones and made a few notes about their location. With such vague information, the ages of these *Homo erectus* fossils have long been in dispute.

To get more precise estimates of these fossils, geochronologists have returned to the sites in Indonesia where they were found. In the mid-1990s, Carl Swisher, a researcher then at the University of California at Berkeley, traveled with his colleagues to the village of Ngandong in eastern Java to measure the age of *Homo erectus* skulls found there in the 1930s. The Ngandong skulls were thought to be a few hundred thousand years old at most, but no one could say just how old they were. Searching through the layer of rock where the *Homo erectus* fossils had been discovered, Swisher's team found teeth of elephants and antelope. They determined the age of the teeth with a method called electron spin resonance, which measures how much radiation damage has accumulated in a fossil. They estimated that the teeth—and, by extension, the *Homo erectus* fossils—were between 27,000 and 53,000 years old.

This was a stunning date. Here was a hominid that was profoundly different from living humans, whose ancestors may have branched off from our own over 1.8 million years ago. If Swisher and his colleagues were right, it might well have existed in Indonesia long after our own species had arrived in the region. Swisher's estimate was met by great skepticism, with some critics suggesting that the Ngandong fossils were actually much older, but had been pushed into the younger deposits where Swisher's team found their mammal teeth. In spite of the criticism, Swisher and his colleagues still maintain that the majority of evidence points to a young age for *Homo erectus*.

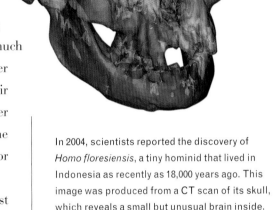

In 2004, scientists reported the discovery of *Homo floresiensis*, a tiny hominid that lived in Indonesia as recently as 18,000 years ago. This image was produced from a CT scan of its skull, which reveals a small but unusual brain inside.

The Ngandong fossils weren't the last surprise Indonesia had to offer. In 1998, researchers working on the Indonesian island of Flores discovered 800,000-year-old stone tools, presumably made by *Homo erectus*. The hominids might have been swept to the island on trees uprooted by floods or tsunamis, or—more tantalizingly—they might have arrived by boat. No one had thought *Homo erectus* had the mental capacity necessary for boat building, and so researchers from Indonesia and Australia redoubled their efforts to find more hominid remains.

But what they found completely surprised them, and the world was just as stunned when they announced their discovery in 2004. While digging through a Flores cave, the scientists found the remains of tiny hominids that would have

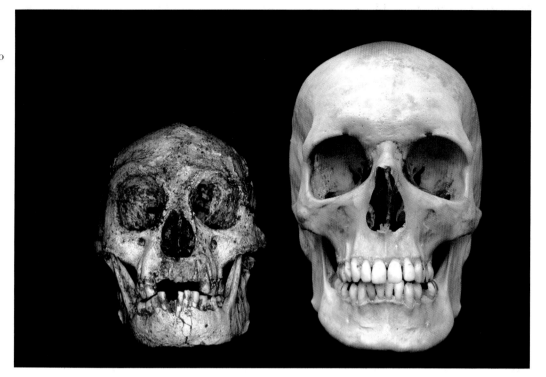

Skulls of *Homo floresiensis* (left) and *Homo sapiens* (right). Scientists believe that the two species share a common ancestor that lived some two million years ago.

stood only three feet high. The researchers discovered one skull among the remains, which indicates that the hominids had a brain that was 417 cubic centimeters, less than a third of our own and roughly the size of a chimpanzee's. And most astonishing of all, the fossils are practically brand new. They range in age from about 95,000 years ago to only 18,000 years ago.

These little fossils—dubbed *Homo floresiensis*—are now the subject of one of the fiercest controversies in hominid evolution. Some paleoanthropologists think that they were actually *Homo sapiens* pygmies. These researchers dismiss the small brain as a case of microcephaly—a birth defect caused by mutations to genes such as ASPM. But the discoverers of the fossils reject this suggestion. Human pygmies have evolved their short stature with genes that cut off their supply of growth hormone. But they only stop growing after their brains have reached adult size. *Homo floresiensis*'s brain is not only far smaller than any *Homo sapiens* brain, but it also has a drastically different shape than ours. That shape—along with other anatomical details—suggests that *Homo floresiensis* was more closely related to *Homo erectus*.

It's possible that full-sized *Homo erectus* arrived on Flores at some point, and then adapted to life on the island. Islands frequently foster the evolution of dwarf animals. Flores, for example, was home to dwarf elephants. It's possible that the limited space on small islands and the lack of competition and predators favors the small. For the first time, hominids may have fallen under the same rule.

Sometimes life on an island causes animals to evolve smaller nervous systems. It seems that hominids have as well. *Homo floresiensis*'s brain shrank down to the smallest size *ever* found in a hominid. Yet when scientists made a CT scan of the *H. floresiensis* brain case, they did not find a degenerate brain inside. In fact, certain regions of the cerebral cortex were enlarged. One of these enlarged areas is also enlarged in the human brain; known as Brodmann's area 10, it is important for planning and initiating actions. *Homo floresiensis* may have had a brain roughly the size of a chimpanzee's, but it may well have had some mental powers more like our own.

Sometimes debates over human origins can never be resolved because the required evidence has vanished forever. Fortunately, there's hope that the debate over *Homo floresiensis* can be settled in the near future. The fossils are so young that the prospects are good to find DNA in them. If *Homo floresiensis* were actually just human pygmies, then their DNA should reflect that. You'd expect it to be most similar to the DNA of Southeast Asian populations. But if *Homo floresiensis* is a descendant of *Homo erectus*, that would mean that it is a very distant cousin to our own species. Its DNA would be even less like our own than Neanderthal DNA.

This test would have huge implications. If *Homo floresiensis* is in fact a separate species, it would mean that we were sharing the planet with at least one other hominid as recently as 18,000 years ago. Our solitary existence today as the only remaining species of hominids would become an extraordinarily recent fluke.

Exactly what drove *Homo floresiensis* to extinction no one can yet say. One possibility is a volcanic eruption that occurred 12,000 years ago. On the other hand, modern humans also began leaving traces of their existence on Flores 11,000 years ago. It is possible that *Homo sapiens* outcompeted their cousins on Flores, much as they did in Europe when they encountered Neanderthals. *Homo erectus* likewise doesn't seem to have survived human contact long.

Manmade extinctions have only become a worry in recent decades, as humans endanger an increasing number of species through hunting, pollution, deforestation and other activities. But extinctions are nothing new. In fact, some scientists now argue that our species became an agent of extinction as it swept across the world and encountered animals that had had no time to adapt to us. In Australia, the ancestors of today's aborigines may have wiped out giant kangaroos and other marsupials. In New Zealand, human settlers hunted the moa, a ten-foot-tall flightless bird, and eradicated the species in a few centuries. When East Asians made their way into the New World approximately 20,000 years ago, they appear to have wiped out the mammoths and many other large mammals.

It would be ironic indeed if it turned out that three of the first species to encounter the sharp blade of our competitive edge were our closest relatives.

A reconstruction of the head of a female *Homo floresiensis.* In life, she would have stood three feet high.

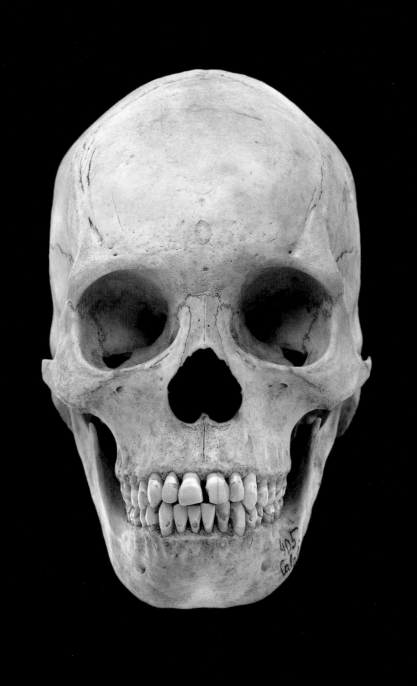

## CHAPTER EIGHT

# WHERE DO WE GO FROM HERE?

Have we reached the end of the story? We've certainly covered a lot of ground. We began with our early primate ancestors leaping through the trees sixty million years ago, raced forward to the dawn of apes, and then followed one ape lineage as its members began to walk upright. Much later our hominid ancestors began to craft stone tools and then embarked on the first of many journeys out of Africa. Forests retreated, deserts expanded, glaciers rose and melted back. Hominid brains grew in fits and starts, hominid tools became more elaborate, and finally our ancestors had acquired all of the fundamental ingredients of modern human existence by about 50,000 years ago.

Our species has not undergone any awesome evolutionary transition since then. An extra pair of eyes has not evolved on our foreheads. We have not sprouted wings. Our lives may be very different today from those of the first *Homo sapiens*, but our anatomy—including the size and shape of our brains—is practically identical. It may seem strange that natural selection, which has produced so many impressive adaptations, would slack off this way. But natural selection is not some sort of conscious engineer, forever creating designs from scratch. It merely tinkers with genes and the bodies made by genes, sometimes generating new innovations and sometimes leaving well enough alone.

A skull of a modern human.

Natural selection has not done away with the many vestiges of past adaptations that were already obsolete millions of years before our species emerged. Our backs, for example, were originally adapted for supporting a four-legged body. They have not adapted very well to our upright existence, leaving us hobbled by slipped disks and pinched nerves. As we've seen, the human brain has been the subject of natural selection as well. Many psychologists now wonder if they can get a deeper understanding of the mind by investigating how it has evolved. The human brain expanded enormously over the past two million years, but our ancestors spent the vast majority of that time not in cities or on farms but in wandering bands of foragers, scavengers and hunters. Our brains may have become finely tuned to that sort of life, and we may still inherit those adaptations.

A new breed of scientists who call themselves evolutionary psychologists are now searching for signs of our hominid heritage in the modern mind. Many of them focus on how men and women behave toward one another. In many cultures, for example, men tend to be attracted to women with large breasts, narrow waists and wide hips. Evolutionary psychologists argue that this is not merely the product of how men are raised, but an evolutionary adaptation. A 2004 study offered some support for this idea, finding that women with large breasts and narrow waists had hormone levels indicating they were more fertile than other women. Men may have evolved an attraction to these features because it brought them more reproductive success.

Emotions may have been shaped by natural selection as well. Evolutionary psychologists have proposed, for example, that jealousy emerged out of the long-term bonds that eventually emerged among hominid parents. They had to invest many years together to raise their children, which made the prospect of being

The human skeleton, like the rest of the human body, is the product of natural selection tinkering with an ancient anatomy. As a result, our bodies are full of oddities and imperfections.

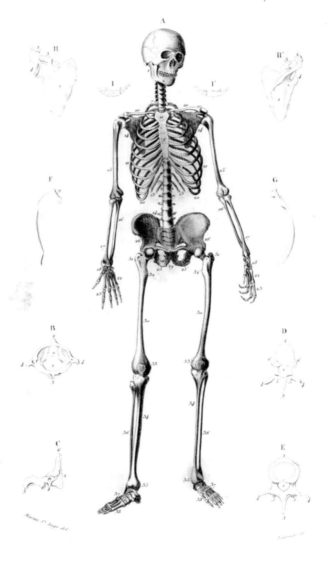

1er Ordre PRIMATES. *BIMANES. Homme.* Ostéologie.

abandoned by one's partner a potential disaster. Hominids may have become very sensitive to signs that might foretell abandonment—a sensitivity we now call jealousy.

Evolution has not only shaped human emotion, evolutionary psychologists argue, but human reasoning as well. They point out that people do badly on certain kinds of logic puzzles if the puzzles are presented abstractly. Here's an example of one of these tough puzzles: a psychologist presents you with four cards, each with a number on one side and a letter on the other. The cards are marked D, F, 3 and 5 respectively. The psychologist then says that if a card has a D on one side, then the other side should be marked with a 3. Which cards do you have to turn over to see if the rule actually holds? The answer is D and 5.

This puzzle becomes much easier if it is expressed in terms of people and social rules. For example, the cards might have information about four people drinking in a bar. One side of a card would be the age of a drinker and the other side would show their drink. Imagine that you are shown four cards that show beer, soda, 25 and 17 respectively. Which cards do you need to turn over to make sure that no one under 21 is drinking alcohol?

Many people get the right answer (in this case, beer and 17). Evolutionary psychologists argue that we do much better with social puzzles because they tap into a faculty that evolved in our hominid ancestors. They lived in small groups that had to share meat and other food. If cheaters broke the rules of a group, the effects could be devastating. As a result, hominids evolved a keen instinct for detecting cheaters.

While our minds may still be attuned to an ancient way of life, we have not stopped evolving. As *Homo sapiens* spread across the planet, new mutations continued to emerge, spread and disappear. Humans carried some of these mutations with them across continents and oceans. Deciphering this genetic history isn't easy, because all living humans descend from only a few thousand Africans. Even smaller groups made the initial migrations out of Africa, becoming the earliest ancestors of Asians and Europeans. These tiny groups gave rise to the six billion people living on Earth today, and did so in only a few thousand generations. That hasn't been long enough for our species to accrue many genetic differences. The wildebeest in Kenya alone have twice as much genetic variation as our entire species. Yet despite this genetic similarity, our species is not just a collection of six billion clones. People vary. They have different skin colors and body shapes. A drug can have a different effect on your body depending on your ancestry.

When most people think of human variations, they think of race. But it's important to bear in mind that the concept of human races was created in the 1700s and 1800s, long before it was possible to look at human variation at the genetic level. It was built instead of a crude mix of observation and chauvinism. The eighteenth-century naturalist Carolus Linnaeus, for example, divided humans into seven races, including *Homo sapiens europeanus* and *Homo sapiens afer* (Africans). He claimed that *Homo sapiens europeanus*'s distinguishing traits included not just white skin but also long flowing hair, blue eyes, a muscular body and a capacity for invention and for governing by laws. The distinguishing traits of *Homo sapiens afer*, by contrast, were black skin, as well as cunning and a personality ruled by impulse. This sort of racism, which has no real basis in biology or behavior, has provided justification for slavery, Nazi genocide and many other great evils over the past 200 years.

Despite this dubious history, scientists today are keenly interested in human genetic variation. It can not only tell us about human history but also shed light on how different genes predispose people to cancer and other diseases. One important measure of diversity is the amount of genetic variation found within a population and between populations. According to the latest studies on the DNA of Africans, Europeans and Asians, only about 15 percent of genetic variation exists between these groups, while 85 percent can be found within them.

While the differences between populations may be small, that doesn't mean they are insignificant. Human populations vary enough, for example, to let geneticists determine where a person's ancestors are from. In 2003, University of Utah geneticists proved this by scanning the human genome for short sequences that tend to vary a lot between people. These stretches of DNA, known as Alu sequences, are prone to harmless mutations, which means that natural selection doesn't remove them from our species. The scientists identi-

Living humans vary in color, shape and size. Yet compared to other primates, human genetic variation is minor.

fied 100 Alu markers and then gathered them from the DNA of 107 sub-Saharan Africans, 67 East Asians and 81 Western Europeans. The individuals in each group shared an almost identical set of markers. The differences between the groups were so clear that the researchers could predict an individual's ancestry with nearly 100 percent accuracy.

Some of the genetic differences between ethnic groups are little more than statistical flukes. To understand why, imagine a country in which people have all sorts of eye colors—brown, blue, hazel, green, grey, pink, purple. Fifty of them board a ship to colonize a distant island. As a random sample of their country's population, they bring with them the full spectrum of eye colors. A few miles from the island shore, the ship sinks in a storm, and only three people make it ashore. By pure luck, they all have purple eyes. The survivors manage to make a life for themselves, and their descendants quickly fill up the entire island. When visitors come to the island, they are shocked to find that the residents all have

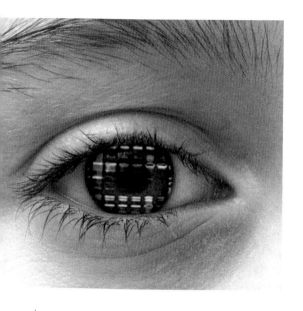

Traits such as eye color are determined by genes. But that doesn't mean that a particular person's eye color must be the product of natural selection.

purple eyes. They might speculate on what sort of advantage purple eyes offered the islanders so that natural selection favored them so strongly. But the real cause was the random hand of fate at work in the shipwreck. The random hand of fate—technically called genetic drift—is a powerful force in recent human history. Humans have migrated around the entire world, often in small numbers. Those small numbers boost some genes at random and eliminate others.

On the other hand, recent research has indicated that some differences between groups of people are not the random hand of fate, but the result of natural selection. In some cases, natural selection may alter the DNA of an enclave of people who live in a small region. In others, it operates across an entire continent.

The most obvious example of natural selection is skin color. The earliest hominids were probably covered mostly in hair, as living apes are. This hair covering became a liability when hominids began walking upright through open landscapes, because it trapped too much heat. Natural selection favored a hairless body instead, along with extra sweat glands to help cool the skin.

But a hairless body brought its own hazards. Underneath the dark coat of an ape, its skin is actually quite pale. Hairless hominids would have become vulnerable to ultraviolet radiation from the high tropical sun. In addition to causing skin cancer, intense ultraviolet light can break down an essential nutrient in the skin called folic acid. Without enough folic acid, men may become infertile and women may give birth to babies with fatal neurological defects. Nina Jablonski and George Chaplin at the California Academy of Sciences have argued that once hominids became hairless, natural selection favored ultraviolet-absorbing pigments that turned their skin dark.

But when dark-skinned humans began migrating away from equatorial Africa, the evolutionary balance shifted. While too much ultraviolet light is dangerous, too little ultraviolet light is also bad for you. That's because it helps our bodies produce vitamin D. Without enough ultraviolet exposure, vitamin D levels fall, which can lead to devastating bone deformities. In regions of the world with low levels of ultraviolet rays, black skin might do its job too well.

Jablonksi and Chaplin argue that the balance between protecting folic acid and synthesizing vitamin D favored darker skins where ultraviolet exposure is high, and paler skins closer to the poles. They've found that the worldwide pattern of skin color matches pretty well with their predictions. There are exceptions, but most seem to prove the rule rather than undermine it. People with the "wrong" skin color tend to belong to groups who have migrated long distances within the past few thousand years. The light-brown Khoisan people of Southern Africa have lived there for tens of thousands of years; darker Zulu people came from tropical Africa much more recently. Eskimos ought to be as pale as Scandinavians, but they arrived in the Arctic only a few thousand years ago, and because they get an unusually rich supply of vitamin D from a diet heavy in fish, natural selection may not create as much of an advantage for pale-skinned Eskimos.

Natural selection has produced other differences between peoples that are less obvious, but no less significant. In 2004, Douglas Wallace of the University of California at Irvine and his colleagues reported signs of natural selection in

Evidence from DNA suggests that humans adapted to the harsh, cold climate of Siberia by evolving the ability to produce more heat from the food they eat.

human mitochondria—the fuel-generating factories of the cell. Mitochondria convert the glucose in food into a compound called adenosine triphosphate (ATP), which the cell can then use as fuel as it crawls around, produces hormones or performs some other task. The production of ATP releases heat as a byproduct, which can help keep our bodies warm.

Studying over 1,000 people, Wallace and his colleagues discovered that people in Europe and northeastern Siberia have inherited unusual mutations in their mitochondrial DNA that can't be found in the genes of Africans. These mutations appear to make European and Siberian mitochondria produce more heat. Wallace and his colleagues suggest that these mutations brought benefits to humans as they moved into cold climates.

In these cases, humans have simply adapted to their physical surroundings just as other animals have. But some recent human adaptations are unusual, because they are the product of our own cultural evolution. As humans invented new ways of surviving, they altered the evolutionary landscape, encouraging the spread of genes that were previously rare. The best-documented example of culture driving biology this way occurred roughly 10,000 years ago, as humans in Europe, parts of Africa and a few other regions began to domesticate cows.

Cattle herding provided people with an immediate benefit in the form of a reliable supply of meat. Cows also produce milk, which is a good source of nutrition, but the first cattle herders probably couldn't drink much of it. As infants, most mammals digest their mothers' milk with the help of a protein they produce, called lactase. Acting as a set of molecular scissors, lactase snips apart a sugar found in milk, called lactose. Once it is cut into pieces, lactose can be absorbed into the bloodstream. But as mammals grow older, they stop producing lactase, with the result that they can no longer digest milk. Humans started out the same way, and many humans today remain lactose intolerant. They get indigestion when they try to drink milk or eat cheese.

But many people who descend from traditional cattle herders can still digest lactose. That's because they have inherited a mutation to a gene called LCT. Scientists are not yet sure how the mutant version of LCT works, but it shows clear signs of having undergone natural selection in the past few thousand years (in fact, it's the strongest selection yet measured in humans). It appears that thousands of years ago, the LCT mutation randomly emerged in cattle-herding people.

# Genetic Engineering: A New Kind of Evolution?

Could genetic engineering alter the future of human evolution? Some observers of recent advances in biotechnology worry that it might. For years now, scientists have been inserting new genes into bacteria, turning them into factories to produce proteins. More recently, scientists have inserted genes into plants and animals. And they've begun to experiment with inserting genes into the cells of humans, in the hopes of curing disorders, such as cystic fibrosis, which are caused by defective genes. The typical procedure for this so-called gene therapy is to load a working copy of the gene in question into a harmless virus. Researchers then inject the virus into the part of the body where the gene is supposed to make proteins. The virus invades the patient's cells and inserts its code into the cell's genome, along with the engineered gene.

While gene therapy has yet to be proven safe and effective, it has already inspired some speculations about where this sort of science could go. For now, gene therapy is targeted at cells in the bodies of children or adults. If these people were to have children of their own, they might pass the same faulty copy of a gene that made them sick in the first place. Now imagine that a man with cystic fibrosis and his wife provide their egg and sperm to a doctor. The doctor lets the fertilized egg divide into four cells, and then transfers one of the eggs to another dish, where it multiplies into a colony.

The doctor loads up viruses with working versions of the gene and sets them loose on the colony. She then searches the dish for a cell that has successfully absorbed the gene.

This cell can no longer give rise to an embryo, but its altered DNA can. The doctor simply has to take the DNA out of the cell. Next, she goes back to one of the three remaining cells from the original embryo, and replaces its DNA with the DNA from the altered cell. With the right combination of signals, this new cell will start dividing again and produce an embryo. When it grows into an adult, that person will carry working copies of the gene in every single cell, including his or her sex cells. Theoretically, his or her descendants will never have to worry about inheriting cystic fibrosis again.

This procedure—called germ line modification—might make it possible not only to repair defective genes but also to give children enhanced genes. Imagine two parents who are short, and are convinced that being tall will give their child an advantage in life. Rather than give their child injections of growth hormone, they might have a doctor install extra copies of the genes that produce the hormone. Intelligence is partly a result of the genes we inherit; if scientists manage to identify some of the most important genes associated with intelligence, it might be possible to engineer children with versions of those genes to make them smarter.

Of course, none of this will happen tomorrow. Today scientists are still struggling to get gene therapy to work. But in twenty years, society may face the choice of altering its future genetic profile. Some people have argued that ethical concerns will keep germ line modification rare. But its attractions may convince many people that they should set their qualms aside. Consider, for example, the fact that scientists are now identifying the genes that produce longevity in animals. Imagine that a doctor offered to add these genes to your children's genomes to ensure that they were healthy and happy into their eighties. Would you say no?

Some skeptics have argued that even if germ line modification did prove successful, it would remain so expensive that only a handful of wealthy people would be able to afford it. Yet new technologies often have a way of becoming affordable. Consider how widespread in-vitro fertilization has become in just twenty-five years. During World War II, antibiotics were precious and rare—so much so that the United States government held onto the country's entire supply in order to treat wounded soldiers. Now, sixty years later, you can walk into a store in a city such as Lagos or Jakarta and buy antibiotics for a few dollars.

If genetic engineering did become widespread, its effects on the human gene pool would be carried forward from one generation to the next. It's an open question whether its effects would amount to short-lived ripples or major waves. The most likely people to use germ line modification at first—wealthy people—also tend to have small families. By definition then, their

Will biotechnology alter our future evolution?

genes would not be favored by natural selection. What's more, genetic modification could turn out to have hidden dangers that emerge only after several generations, which would also make these genes grow rare. On the other hand, engineered genes could spread if natural selection strongly favors them. A lethal virus might emerge from a disturbed rain forest, and the only way to survive might be to carry a man-made resistance gene.

In the end, the only way to know would be to run an experiment. And given the advances in genetic engineering these days, it looks as if the experiment is about to begin.

It somehow disabled the off-switch for lactase production, and allowed people who carried it to drink milk into adulthood. The extra calories and protein from the milk ultimately translated into extra children for people who had the mutation. Mutations to LCT may have cropped up among people who did not herd cattle, but they offered no benefit because there was no cow's milk for them to drink.

Culture has shaped human evolution not only with the benefits it has brought, but also with new threats. The most common form of malaria, for example, has thrived since humans invented agriculture. This strain of malaria is caused by a single-celled mosquito-dwelling parasite called *Plasmodium falciparum*. Originally *Plasmodium*-carrying mosquitoes lived in African forests and drank the blood of forest animals. But over the past few thousand years they moved into the fields that African farmers began to clear for crops. They laid their eggs in the stagnant water that puddled in the fields, and feasted on the blood of farmers as they slept. The parasite's numbers exploded, and eventually it hitchhiked with mosquitoes into southern Europe and southern Asia. Finally humans brought it to the New World. Today malaria causes over a million deaths a year, mostly in Africa where it began.

Nothing speeds up evolution faster than disease, because any mutation that can provide some resistance may save an animal from death. We humans are no exception. By unwittingly unleashing malaria, our ancestors triggered an explosion of evolution not only in *Plasmodium* but in our own species as well. Throughout malaria's range, human populations have acquired new defenses against the parasite, blocking its entry into blood cells to break its life cycle.

From defenses against diseases to protection from cold climates, the evolution of our species continued even after the dawn of modern human life 50,000 years ago. Is it possible to project forward and predict what evolution will do to *Homo sapiens* over the next 50,000 years?

Evolution has acted on humans over just the past few thousand years. A number of cultures, such as the Maasai of East Africa, took up cattle herding. As a result, natural selection favored mutations in their genes that allowed them to digest milk.

Certainly not. Human culture now alters the rules by which biological evolution unfolds. The future of human culture will therefore help steer the course of evolution. In order to predict the future of our species, we have to predict the future of our society. That's no small task, when you consider that we can't predict what the stock market will do next week.

Still, scientists have indulged in some speculation about what the future will

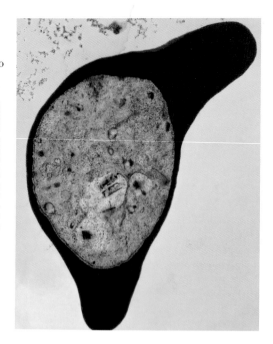

A human red blood cell plays host to *Plasmodium*, the parasite that causes malaria. Humans have been subject to malaria for thousands of years, and its deadliness has driven the evolution of many adaptations to fight the parasite.

bring. Some have looked at human evolution up close, on the generation-by-generation scale. They have pointed out that natural selection works fastest when there are big differences in the sizes of families. Some genes may allow some people to produce seven children, while alternate versions might leave them childless— or even dead before they have a chance to have children. Antibiotics, clean drinking water, steady supplies of food and other pleasures of modern life have blunted the knife that cleaves the species. Genes that leave people prone to juvenile diabetes or other potentially fatal disorders are no longer a guarantee against having children. Meanwhile, large families are becoming rarer as the rate of population growth slows. In fact, the world's population is now projected to level off at about nine billion by 2100. If the unconscious competition between genes is leading to much smaller payoffs for the winners, the race itself may be slowing down.

On the other hand, the world today is hardly free of diseases. In just the past thirty years, HIV has exploded into one of the worst epidemics in recorded history. It has killed over twenty million people and shows every sign of continuing its deadly march. Certain genes offer protection to HIV, just as certain genes offer protection to malaria. Unless we can stop the spread of HIV, the virus will shift the genetic profile of our species. It's likely that new diseases will continue to put pressure on our genome. HIV is believed to have evolved from chimpanzee viruses, which hopped to our species as logging roads were cut into African forests, making it possible for hunters to slaughter more chimps and other primates. Many other viruses could colonize us by a similar route.

While parasites will continue to cause enormous suffering to our species, we probably don't have to worry about them causing complete extinction. Diseases can wipe out species with small ranges, but there's no evidence they can cause the extinction of widespread animals. But the history of life offers many warnings to us. An asteroid impact sixty-five million years ago may have wiped out the dinosaurs. A sudden surge in global warming 250 million years ago claimed 90 percent of all species on Earth.

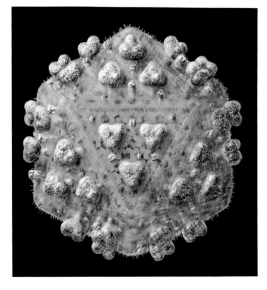

Artist's rendition of HIV, the virus that causes AIDS. HIV has become a major cause of death in humans in just the past three decades. Unless its spread is stopped soon, the virus will probably influence the future evolution of our species.

While these gloomy possibilities can't be ignored, that doesn't mean that they are our destiny. Perhaps we will manage to bring diseases under control, ward off asteroids with interplanetary mines and find a way to keep our emissions of greenhouse gases from scorching us. But even in a sunnier, extinction-free future, our species would probably keep evolving. One particularly fascinating possibility is that our species will give rise to a new one.

It would be a most unusual birth, as species go. The best documented way for a new species to emerge is for a population to become physically isolated from the rest of its species—cut off by a river, for example, or swept away to an island. The isolated population evolves for thousands of years, acquiring mutations that the rest of the species lacks. If the population can then mix with the rest of the species—if, for example, dropping sea levels turn its island into a peninsula—its new mutations may prevent any successful interbreeding. For many biologists, that's the hallmark of a new species.

It's hard to imagine how humans could become physically isolated long enough somewhere on Earth to form a new species—as long as there are ships in the sea and planes in the air. But there may be one way that a new species of human might emerge on a peaceful, intermingled Earth. Geneticist Matt Hurles of the Sanger Center in England and his colleagues point out that as the human population approaches nine billion, some of evolution's rules may change in subtle but important ways.

It helps to think back to the island of purple-eyed shipwreck survivors. The fatal shipwreck not only boosted the number of purple-eye genes on the island but completely eliminated the genes for other eye colors. If shipwrecks and other statistical flukes wiped out enough people with brown eyes, the gene for brown eyes would vanish from our species altogether. A species that is made up of small populations is prone to these sorts of statistical flukes, which can wipe out genes. As a result, it ends up with low levels of genetic diversity.

But in big populations—say, a population of nine billion humans—these statistical flukes have a much weaker effect. There are always enough brown-eyed people to spread the brown-eye gene to the next generation. Hurles and his colleagues suggest that in the future, the large size of the human population will foster a rise in mutations in the human genome. These mutations will for the most part be utterly harmless. But under some conditions, the researchers suggest, they can cause infertility.

People can become infertile because their sperm or eggs don't form properly. Normally, sex cells form from precursor cells equipped with the standard allotment of twenty-three pairs of chromosomes. As the precursor cells divide, so do the chromosome pairs, so that each sex cell winds up with only one chromosome from each pair. But before the chromosome pairs part ways, they have time for a final embrace. During this hug, they swap similar chunks of DNA. This embrace only occurs because the chromosomes are so similar that they can lock together. If their sequences are too different, they cannot line up properly. The dance of cell division is thrown off, and the sex cells that are produced as a result may wind up with an extra chromosome. These malformed cells will not be able to produce a fertilized egg.

Now imagine nine billion people with a vast number of mutations in their genomes. The mismatching of chromosomes becomes common, and widespread infertility follows. Hurles and his colleagues suggest that people whose parents had the same genetic background would have the lowest risk of infertility. That's because the chromosomes they inherited from their parents would tend to have the same mutations, and thus line up properly. Human genes would no longer get mixed together as much as they do today. Instead, people would begin to form populations that were reproductively isolated. If this isolation lasted for thousands of years, one of these populations might evolve into a separate species.

All of this speculation—and speculation is what it must remain—deals with the future of biological evolution, the sort that has driven life's history for some four billion years. But it may turn out that biology may not drive the next stage of human evolution. Humans have developed the cultural traditions of their ape ancestors into a high-speed evolutionary process of their own. Our ideas spread, change and give rise to new ideas. They don't need millions of years to transform. It's rare for a few months to go by without some new electronic device hitting the

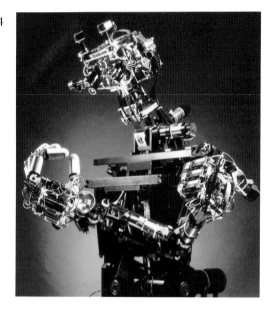

Cog, a robot built by scientists at the Massachusetts Institute of Technology, is designed to experience the world in much the way a human being does. It raises the unsettling possibility that machines may carry on our evolution.

market. Those devices still need us to conceive of them, build them, program them and debug them. But perhaps not for long. It is possible that self-replicating artificial systems will emerge. If we program them with our culture, they could carry the ideas of our species into a new sort of existence—one that might even spread to other worlds. Some futurists have speculated that this is a common pattern for intelligent life throughout the universe. Once a species becomes intelligent enough to build tools, it's only a matter of time before it passes into a post-biological civilization. By this line of reasoning, our best chance of detecting signs of extraterrestrial life is not to search for habitable planets, but for self-replicating machines wandering through deep space.

If we find them, we might be looking at our future.

# FURTHER READING

## GENERAL BOOKS ON HUMAN EVOLUTION

Boyd, R. and J.B. Silk. *How Humans Evolved.* New York: Norton, 2002.

Dawkins, R. *The Ancestor's Tale: A Pilgrimage to the Dawn of Evolution.* Boston: Houghton Mifflin, 2004.

Johanson, D.C. and B. Edgar. *From Lucy to Language.* New York: Simon & Schuster, 1996.

Klein, R.G. *The Human Career: Human Biological and Cultural Origins.* Chicago: University of Chicago Press, 1999.

Lewin, R. and R. Foley. *Principles of Human Evolution.* Malden, Massachusetts: Blackwell, 2004.

Tattersall, I. and J.H. Schwartz. *Extinct Humans.* Boulder, Colorado: Westview Press, 2000.

de Waal, F.B.M. *Tree of Origin: What Primate Behavior Can Tell Us about Human Social Evolution.* Cambridge, Massachusetts: Harvard University Press, 2001.

Zimmer, C. *Evolution: The Triumph of an Idea.* New York: HarperCollins, 2001.

## CHAPTER ONE: THE CLUES

Darwin, C. *The Descent of Man, and Selection in Relation to Sex.* London: J. Murray, 1871.

Huxley, T.H. *Man's Place in Nature.* Mineola, New York: Dover Publications, 2003.

Paley, W. *Natural Theology; or, Evidences of the Existence and Attributes of the Deity.* London: Printed for J. Faulder, 1809.

## CHAPTER TWO: A BUDDING BRANCH

Brunet, M., F. Guy et al. "A New Hominid from the Upper Miocene of Chad, Central Africa." *Nature* 418 (2002): 145–51.

Glazko, G.V. and M. Nei. "Estimation of Divergence Times for Major Lineages of Primate Species." *Molecular Biology and Evolution* 20 (2003): 424–34.

Haile-Selassie, Y., G. Suwa et al. "Late Miocene Teeth from Middle Awash, Ethiopia, and Early Hominid Dental Evolution." *Science* 303 (2004): 1503–5.

Lewin, R. *Bones of Contention: Controversies in the Search for Human Origins.* Chicago: University of Chicago Press, 1997.

Vignaud, P., P. Duringer et al. "Geology and Palaeontology of the Upper Miocene Toros-Menalla Hominid Locality, Chad." *Nature* 418 (2002): 152–55.

White, T.D., G. Suwa et al. "*Australopithecus ramidus,* a New Species of Early Hominid from Aramis, Ethiopia." *Nature* 371 (1994): 306–12.

Wood, B. "Hominid Revelations from Chad." *Nature* 418 (2002): 133–35.

## CHAPTER THREE: THE WALK BEGINS

Bonnefille, R., R. Potts et al. "High-resolution Vegetation and Climate Change Associated with Pliocene *Australopithecus afarensis.*" *Proceedings of the National Academy of Sciences* USA 101 (2004): 12125–29.

Corruccini, R.S. and H.M. McHenry. "Knuckle-walking Hominid Ancestors." *Journal of Human Evolution* 40 (2001): 507–11

Nagano, A., B.R. Umberger et al. "Neuromusculoskeletal Computer Modeling and Simulation of Upright, Straight-legged, Bipedal Locomotion of *Australopithecus afarensis* (A.L. 288–1)." *American Journal of Physical Anthropology* 126 (2005): 2–13.

Stanford, C.B. *Upright: the Evolutionary Key to Becoming Human*. Boston: Houghton Mifflin, 2003.

Videan, E.N. and W.C. McGrew. "Bipedality in Chimpanzee *(Pan troglodytes)* and Bonobo *(Pan paniscus):* Testing Hypotheses on the Evolution of Bipedalism." *American Journal of Physical Anthropology* 118 (2002): 184–90.

Ward, C. V., M.G. Leakey et al. "Morphology of *Australopithecus anamensis* from Kanapoi and Allia Bay, Kenya." *Journal of Human Evolution* 41 (2001): 255–368.


CHAPTER FOUR: THE TOOLMAKERS

Asfaw, B., W.H. Gilbert et al. "Remains of *Homo erectus* from Bouri, Middle Awash, Ethiopia." *Nature* 416 (2002): 317–20.

Asfaw, B., T. White et al. "*Australopithecus garhi:* A New Species of Early Hominid from Ethiopia." *Science* 284 (1999): 629–35.

Backwell, L.R. and F. d'Errico. "Evidence of Termite Foraging by Swartkrans Early Hominids." *Proceedings of the National Academy of Sciences* USA 98 (2001): 1358–63.

Dominguez-Rodrigo, M., T.R. Pickering et al. "Cutmarked Bones from Pliocene Sites at Gona, Afar, Ethiopia: Implications for the Function of the World's Oldest Stone Tools." *Journal of Human Evolution* 48 (2005): 109–21.

Dunbar, R. "Psychology: Evolution of the Social Brain." *Science* 302 (2003): 1160–1.

Peters, C.R. and J.C. Vogel. "Africa's Wild C(4) Plant Foods and Possible Early Hominid Diets." *Journal of Human Evolution* 48 (2005): 219–36.

Plummer, T. "Flaked Stones and Old Bones: Biological and Cultural Evolution at the Dawn of Technology." *American Journal of Physical Anthropology* Supplement 39 (2004): 118–64.

Potts, R. "Paleoenvironmental Basis of Cognitive Evolution in Great Apes." *American Journal of Primatology* 62 (2004): 209–28.

Semaw, S., M.J. Rogers et al. "2.6-Million-Year-Old Stone Tools and Associated Bones from OGS-6 and OGS-7, Gona, Afar, Ethiopia." *Journal of Human Evolution* 45 (2003): 169–77.

Semaw, S., S.W. Simpson et al. "Early Pliocene Hominids from Gona, Ethiopia." *Nature* 433 (2005): 301–5.

Vallender, E. J. and B.T. Lahn. "Positive Selection on the Human Genome." *Human Molecular Genetics* 13 (2004): R245–54.


CHAPTER FIVE: BECOMING HUMAN

Anton, S.C. "Natural History of *Homo erectus.*" *American Journal of Physical Anthropology* Supplement 37 (2003): 126–70.

Anton, S.C., W.R. Leonard et al. "An Ecomorphological Model of the Initial Hominid Dispersal from Africa." *Journal of Human Evolution* 43 (2002): 773–85.

Bramble, D.M. and D.E. Lieberman. "Endurance Running and the Evolution of *Homo.*" *Nature* 432 (2004): 345–52.

Coqueugniot, H., J.J. Hublin et al. "Early Brain Growth in *Homo erectus* and Implications for Cognitive Ability." *Nature* 431 (2004): 299–302.

Gabunia, L., A. Vekua et al. "Earliest Pleistocene Hominid Cranial Remains from Dmanisi, Republic of Georgia: Taxonomy, Geological Setting, and Age." *Science* 288 (2000): 1019–25.

Hawkes, K. "Grandmothers and the Evolution of Human Longevity." *American Journal of Human Biology* 15 (2003): 380–400.

Jungers, W.L., A.A. Pokempner et al. "Hypoglossal Canal Size in Living *Hominoids* and the Evolution of Human Speech." *American Journal of Human Biology* 75 (2003): 473–84.

Potts, R., A.K. Behrensmeyer et al. "Small Mid-Pleistocene *Hominin* Associated with East African Acheulean Technology." *Science* 305 (2004): 75–8.

Vekua, A., D. Lordkipanidze et al. "A New Skull of Early *Homo* from Dmanisi, Georgia." *Science* 297 (2002): 85–9.

Yamei, H., R. Potts et al. "Mid-Pleistocene Acheulean-like Stone Technology of the Bose Basin, South China." *Science* 287 (2000): 1622–6.

## CHAPTER SIX: SAPIENS

Haile-Selassie, Y., B. Asfaw et al. "Hominid Cranial Remains from Upper Pleistocene Deposits at Aduma, Middle Awash, Ethiopia." *American Journal of Physical Anthropology* 123 (2004): 1–10.

Jobling, M.A., M. Hurles et al. *Human Evolutionary Genetics*. New York: Garland Science, 2004.

Ke, Y., B. Su et al. "African Origin of Modern Humans in East Asia: a Tale of 12,000 Y Chromosomes." *Science* 292 (2001): 1151–3.

McDougall, I., F.H. Brown et al. "Stratigraphic Placement and Age of Modern Humans from Kibish, Ethiopia." *Nature* 433 (2005): 733–6.

Wells, S. and M. Read. *The Journey of Man: A Genetic Odyssey*. Princeton, New Jersey: Princeton University Press, 2002.

White, T.D., B. Asfaw et al. "Pleistocene *Homo sapiens* from Middle Awash, Ethiopia." *Nature* 423 (2003): 742–7.

## CHAPTER SEVEN: THE LAST WAVE

Arsuaga, J.L.D., A. Klatt et al. *The Neanderthal's Necklace: In Search of the First Thinkers*. New York: Four Walls Eight Windows, 2002.

Balter, M. "Paleoanthropology: Small but Smart? Flores Hominid Shows Signs of Advanced Brain." *Science* 307 (2005): 1386–9.

Brown, P., T. Sutikna et al. "A New Small-bodied Hominin from the Late Pleistocene of Flores, Indonesia." *Nature* 431 (2004): 1055–61.

Clark, J.D., Y. Beyene et al. "Stratigraphic, Chronological and Behavioural Contexts of Pleistocene *Homo sapiens* from Middle Awash, Ethiopia." *Nature* 423 (2003): 747–52.

Falk, D., C. Hildebolt et al. "The Brain of LB1, *Homo floresiensis*." *Science* 308 (2005): 242–45.

Finlayson, C. *Neanderthals and Modern Humans: An Ecological and Evolutionary Perspective*. New York: Cambridge University Press, 2004.

McBrearty, S. and A.S. Brooks. "The Revolution That Wasn't: A New Interpretation of the Origin of Modern Human Behavior." *Journal of Human Evolution* 39 (2000): 453–563.

Mellars, P. "Neanderthals and the Modern Human Colonization of Europe." *Nature* 432 (2004): 461–5.

Morwood, M.J., R.P. Soejono et al. "Archaeology and Age of a New *Hominin* from Flores in Eastern Indonesia." *Nature* 431 (2004): 1087–91.

Shea, J. "*Neandertals*, Competition, and the Origin of Modern Human Behavior in the Levant." *Evolutionary Anthropology* 12 (2003): 173–187.

Swisher, C.C., 3rd, W.J. Rink et al. "Latest *Homo erectus* of Java: Potential Contemporaneity with *Homo sapiens* in Southeast Asia." *Science* 274 (1996): 1870–4.

## CHAPTER EIGHT: WHERE DO WE GO FROM HERE?

Bamshad, M.J., S. Wooding et al. "Human Population Genetic Structure and Inference of Group Membership." *American Journal of Human Genetics* 72 (2003): 578–89.

Boyd, R. and P.J. Richerson. *The Origin and Evolution of Cultures.* New York: Oxford University Press, 2004.

Buss, D.M. *Handbook of Evolutionary Psychology.* Hoboken, New Jersey: John Wiley & Sons, 2005.

Harris, C.R. "A Review of Sex Differences in Sexual Jealousy, Including Self-report Data, Psychophysiological Responses, Interpersonal Violence, and Morbid Jealousy." *Personality and Social Psychology Review* 7 (2003): 102–28.

Jablonski, N.G. and G. Chaplin. "The evolution of human skin coloration." *Journal of Human Evolution* 39 (2000): 57–106.

Jasienska, G., A. Ziomkiewicz et al. "Large Breasts and Narrow Waists Indicate High Reproductive Potential In Women." *Proceedings of the Royal Society of London (Biological Sciences)* 271 (2004): 1213–17.

Stock, G. *Redesigning Humans: Our Inevitable Genetic Future.* Boston: Houghton Mifflin, 2002.

Stone, V.E., L. Cosmides et al. "Selective Impairment of Reasoning about Social Exchange in a Patient with Bilateral Limbic System Damage." *Proceedings of the National Academy of Sciences* USA 99 (2002): 11531–6.

Sugiyama, L.S., J. Tooby et al. "Cross-cultural Evidence of Cognitive Adaptations for Social Exchange among the Shiwiar of Ecuadorian Amazonia." *Proceedings of the National Academy of Sciences* USA 99 (2002): 11537–42.

# PICTURE CREDITS

*Every effort has been made to correctly attribute all material reproduced in this book. If errors have unwittingly occurred, we will be happy to correct them in future editions.*

Front cover: Mauricio Anton/National Geographic Image Collection
Back cover: Mission Paléoanthropologique Franco-Tchadienne
Endpapers: © D.J. Maizels, 2005; Courtesy of Sileshi Semaw

*1*: Bettmann/CORBIS
*2*: Courtesy of Kenneth Mowbray and Blaine Maley
*3*: Pascal Goetgheluck/Photo Researchers, Inc.
*6–7*: Illustration by Tadeusz Majewski

## CHAPTER ONE

8: Illustration by MagicGroup s.r.o. (Czech Republic)–www.magicgroup.cz
11: Mission Paléoanthropologique Franco-Tchadienne
12: (Top) Sinclair Stammers/Science Photo Library; (Bottom) Pascal Goetgheluck/Science Photo Library
13: John Reader/Science Photo Library
14: Science Photo Library
15: Tony Camacho/Science Photo Library
16: 1996 David L. Brill/Brill Atlanta
17: 1996 David L. Brill/Brill Atlanta
18: Volker Steger/Science Photo Library
19: Science Photo Library
21: Biophoto Associates/Firstlight.ca
22: © Feenixx, Inc., 2005
23: Alfred Pasieka/Science Photo Library

## CHAPTER TWO

24: Mission Paléoanthropologique Franco-Tchadienne
27: Pascal Goetgheluck/Science Photo Library
28: Illustration by Tadeusz Majewski
30: Illustration by MagicGroup s.r.o. (Czech Republic)–www.magicgroup.cz
31: Barbara Strnadova/Firstlight.ca
32: Photograph courtesy of Frans de Waal from de Waal, *Peacemaking among Primates* (Boston: Harvard University Press, 1989)
35: George Holton/Firstlight.ca
36–37: Pascal Goetgheluck/Science Photo Library
38: Science Photo Library
39: John Reader/Photo Researchers, Inc.
41: Illustration by Tadeusz Majewski
43: Pascal Goetgheluck/Science Photo Library

## CHAPTER THREE

44: © John Gurche
46: Bo Veisland, MI&I/Science Photo Library
48: Pascal Goetgheluck/Photo Researchers, Inc.
49: James Stevenson/Science Photo Library
50: © John Gurche
51: John Reader/Science Photo Library
52: Georg Gerster/Firstlight.ca
53: Renee Lynn/Firstlight.ca
55: John Reader/Science Photo Library
56: Courtesy of R. Savage, PREMOG, Liverpool University
58: Bettmann/CORBIS
59: (Top) B.G. Thomson/Firstlight.ca; (Bottom) John Reader/Science Photo Library

## CHAPTER FOUR

60: © The Natural History Museum, London
63: © The Natural History Museum, London
64: Tom McHugh/Firstlight.ca
65: Tim Flach/Getty Images
66–67: © The Natural History Museum, London

# Index

# ACKNOWLEDGMENTS

I would like to thank the researchers who generously gave their time to me as I explored our origins, including Leslie Aiello, Michel Brunet, Robin Crompton, Matthew Hurles, Richard Klein, Sally McBrearty, William McGrew, Bernard Wood and Joao Zilhao. I would particularly like to thank Robert Boyd, Sileshi Semaw and Chris Stringer for also looking over parts of the manuscript to check its accuracy. Most of all, I want to express my deep gratitude to Tim White for reading the entire manuscript in two of its incarnations. This book had its origins as an article for *Discover*, under the auspices of David Grogan and Steven Petranek.

I would like thank to Don Fehr at Smithsonian Books and everyone at Madison Press Books who made this book more than a collection of words, including Charis Cotter, Wanda Nowakowska and Brian Soye.

Finally and most importantly, I must thank my wife, Grace, for her endless love and support. She makes all my books possible and reminds me why they matter. And I'd like to thank my daughters, Charlotte and Veronica, for not sneaking into my office too often.

*—Carl Zimmer*

Madison Press Books would like to thank Charis Cotter for her dedication in bringing this book to press, Shima Aoki for her picture detective work and Tadeusz Majewski for his inspired illustrations. We are grateful for Linda Gustafson's thoughtful design and Peter Ross's help with the illustrations. We would also like to give special thanks to photographer David Brill and artist John Gurche for their invaluable contributions. Don Fehr of Smithsonian Books supported the project from the beginning with great enthusiasm, and Donna Ruvituso from HarperCollins brought it all together with smooth efficiency. Finally, it was a real pleasure to work with Carl Zimmer, whose combination of knowledge, skill and good humor make him a truly delightful author.

Editorial Director
WANDA NOWAKOWSKA

Project Editor
CHARIS COTTER

Editorial Assistance
SHIMA AOKI

Book Design
COUNTERPUNCH/
LINDA GUSTAFSON

Art Director
JENNIFER LUM

Vice President, Business
Affairs & Production
SUSAN BARRABLE

Production Manager
SANDRA L. HALL

Printed by
TIEN WAH PRESS
SINGAPORE

SMITHSONIAN INTIMATE
GUIDE TO HUMAN ORIGINS
was produced by
MADISON PRESS BOOKS

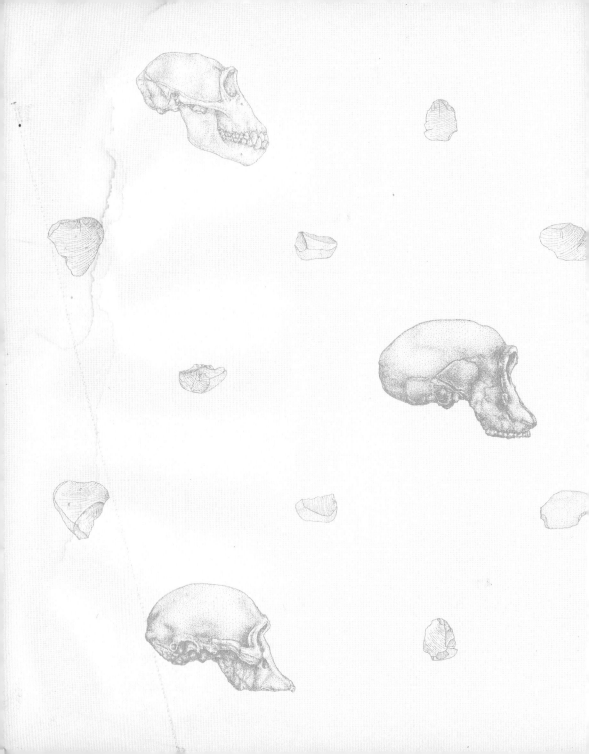